SAILBOARDING
FOR EVERYONE

JEFF TOGHILL

Technical Assistant Bruce Wylie
Photographs by Eve Sheppard

HODDER AND STOUGHTON
LONDON SYDNEY AUCKLAND TORONTO

British Library Cataloguing in Publication Data
Toghill, Jeff
   Sailboarding for everyone.
   1.Windsurfing
   1.Title
   797.3'3   GV811.63W56
   ISBN 0 340 36363 0

Contents

Introduction

There are few participation sports which have as wide an appeal as sailboarding. Kids love it. Teenagers exhaust their youthful energy on it. Mums and dads find it an exciting family sport. And oldies reactivate their waning vigour with it.

I should know. I was over forty when sailboarding gave me a new dimension in life. My children rode on the back of the board from the age of three until they had the strength to raise the rig themselves. My wife took to it like a proverbial duck to water. And our circle of friends widened rapidly as sailboard 'addiction' spread to include the curious as well as the converted.

To most people, flying off the top of a wave at phenomenal speed, or screaming over the surface of a lake in a creditable imitation of Sir Donald Campbell, is just not on. That all requires too much skill, too much energy, too much physical strength.

And they are quite right, for that is the spectacular side of the sport, and only the chosen few ever attain, or even want to attain, those heights. By the same token, it takes enormous skill, energy and strength to race a formula 5000 car around a major raceway circuit, but how many people learn to drive with formula 5000 racing in mind?

Ordinary, everyday sailboarding requires only average skill, modest energy and little physical strength when it is done properly. It is within the reach of everyone, and to those who are addicted, it would seem a major tragedy that some people will go through life without ever having experienced the joys of sailboarding! Indeed, the constant cry of the new enthusiast is: 'Why didn't I do this years ago!'

If patience is a virtue, then budding sailboarders need above all to be virtuous. For patience is the only real requirement of this exhilarating sport. It takes time and perseverance, for early learner days are fraught with frustration. But it can be mastered, and mastered easily. No matter how old or how young you are, how weak or how strong, sailboarding is there for you to enjoy if you have the patience and perseverance.

*Still-water sailboarding caught on quickly on European
lakes.*

1. The Board and Rig

Early origins

Although sailboarding is one of the latest and most modern of water sports, it combines the basic principles of two of the oldest—sailing and surfboard riding. In fact, the first sailboard came into being because a Californian surfing enthusiast felt the need for a further dimension to conventional surfing. Most of the fancy riding and freestyle techniques were part of everyday boardriding and surfing was in danger of losing some of its appeal through lack of variety. With greater leisure time, youngsters were spending more and more time boardriding and were mastering even the advanced techniques in a very short time. A new challenge was needed to maintain interest in the big waves of the surf, and so far no other surf sport had produced such a challenge.

At the same time, a number of young sailing enthusiasts were looking for an added dimension to their sport, and since most still-water activities had been tested and tried, they turned their eyes to the surf. Once again it was a Californian, Hobie Alter, who took sailing into the surf, using a modified catamaran—the now-famous Hobie Cat—to extend the exhilaration of conventional high-flying catamaran sailing in still water to riding surf waves. This exciting machine could sail out through the surf, flying through the top of approaching waves to become almost airborne, then turn and catch a wave back to the beach, racing down the face like a conventional surfboard.

But the Hobie Cat was not the answer to either the sailors' or the surfers' problems. Possibly its rig was too clumsy and complicated and too vulnerable in the surf waves. Possibly it was too heavy and too cumbersome for single-handing in the violent conditions off the beach. Whatever the reason, the Hobie Cat became less of a new surf challenge and more an institution in its own right. Although it is now one of the most exciting of sailing boats, it is used more in still or open water than in the surf.

The obvious need was for a small, surfboard-like craft which was easily handled by one person in sizeable waves, was rugged and was relatively inexpensive. It was with these factors in mind that Californian aeronautical engineer, Jim Drake, set his mind to work in 1961. It was not until 1969 that Drake and fellow Californian, Hoyle Schweitzer, produced an aeronautically designed sailboard—the forerunner of today's craft. Although a sailboard was produced in 1965 by a Pennsylvanian inventor named S. Newman Darby, this was a square-rigged version that did not catch on. It was Drake's and Schweitzer's design that produced the first real sailing and surfing challenge. It was the first model of the now internationally acclaimed Windsurfer.

The sport catches on

Although sailboarding originated in California, and although it was designed as a surf sport, it did not find popularity in the United States of America or with other surfing nations. Paradoxically, it first became popular in the sheltered lakes of Europe where neither the water temperature nor the conditions are ideal for sailboarding.

Since 1970, Drake and Schweitzer had struggled to get the sport accepted in California, but with limited success. Then a Dutch manufacturer, Nijverdal Ten Cate, began to manufacture Windsurfers in Europe under license from the Americans. Immediately the sport caught on. Although there is virtually no surf in northern Europe, and the climate limits any sort of water activities to a few months of the year, sailboarding became the 'in' sport and rival manufacturers sprang up like mushrooms. Within five years, some 150 000 sailboards were cleaving the waters around the continent, and the sport was well established.

Although they were slow in getting under way, the Californians soon caught up. The perfect climate and surf of the West Coast made for an ideal spawning ground and new sailboards began to appear in profusion, their brightly coloured sails sparkling across every surf beach and every estuary along the Californian coast. Other surf-loving countries soon succumbed to the exhilarating addiction of the sailboard and the multi-coloured rash spread through Australia and New Zealand, South Africa, South America and back to its origins in Europe and Britain.

Developments of the early designs added further dimensions to the original use of the sailboard so that today it can be enjoyed on almost any type of waterway in the world in a variety of sailing activities. Fast planing boards still skim effortlessly across the glassy lake surfaces in Europe, while in Hawaii, waveboards rocket into the sky from the top of huge surf waves like colourful Polaris missiles.

Types of boards

With such a variety of sailing conditions it follows that there must be a variety of boards to handle them. In addition, numerous different types of

boards are necessary to cope with different degrees of sailing skills. Although a standard 'still-water' sailboard can be used in moderate surf waves, it will perform badly and give the rider a hard time. Similarly, a top-performance wave-jumping board is not the vehicle on which to learn sailboarding.

Boards therefore come in a variety of shapes, sizes and rigs to cater for every sailboarding requirement. Most modern boards fall into one of the following categories.

Learner boards

Although most beginners learn to sail on a standard board, learner boards are available to make the process a little easier and less frustrating. These boards are mostly wider and more stable than standard boards and thus are less likely to tip over. Similarly, the rig usually has a smaller sail area and may be lighter in construction to allow the beginner to get the hang of raising the rig without straining his or her back.

However, such boards are of little use other than for basic training purposes and are therefore not of great use to the average boardrider. As soon as you have mastered the basic techniques the board is virtually obsolete and thus a waste of

Starting sailing can be frustrating no matter what board you use.

money unless you can hand it on to another beginner. Most learner boards are used in sailboard schools where they can be used *ad infinitum*.

Standard or 'fun' boards

These are the boards designed for riders of average skill, and are used mostly in still water. A standard board is usually about 3.5 metres long and weighs around 18 kilograms, so it can be easily carried by an adult. It is buoyant so that at least one, and sometimes more, persons can stand on it without the board sinking below the surface. It is fairly wide, about 0.7 metre, and thus fairly stable. Most fun boards are responsive and reasonably fast and can be used by beginners as well as by skilled boardriders. Indeed, they are the ideal all-round board and are therefore the most popular.

Different rigs can be obtained to enable the board to be adapted for a number of requirements. For children, who may not have the physical strength to lift the rig from the water or hold it against anything but the lightest breeze, a 'mini' rig is provided. For experts who sail in all weathers, storm rigs with heavier sailcloth and reduced sail area can be fitted or conversely, large, light-weather sails can be used when the breeze dies to a zephyr.

Racing boards

As with all types of sailing, sailboard racing demands greater performance and thus modification of the standard equipment. Racing yachts are designed to move faster through the water by modifications to hull and rig, and much the same applies to racing sailboards. Narrower hulls reduce the friction of wetted surfaces and sharpened bows provide better performance to windward. Fine adjustments of dagger board and sail shape enable the boards' performance to be honed to extract the maximum speed under changing conditions, while different rigs can be designed to improve speed through different wind strengths.

But attaining greater speed always means sacrificing some basic quality, and as a result, few racing boards are suitable for learners or for family fun use.

Wave boards

Wave-jumping and surfing calls for a great deal of foot control, so most sailboards used for this type of activity have footstraps fitted behind the mast. To make them more manoeuvrable, they are usually smaller and lighter than standard boards, and in fact there is a very close resemblance between most wave-jumping boards and the conventional surfboard.

Rigs are also different for wave-jumping. Full-width battens are sometimes fitted to maintain the aerofoil shape in the sail as the board rockets off the top of a wave and catches backwinds. Sail area is usually smaller and the sail cut higher than with standard boards. Most waveboards are low in buoyancy and must be planing across the surface of the water before they will take the full bodyweight of the boardrider. This calls for special sailing techniques.

Fun boards are just that—lots of fun!

< Standard boards can be used for competitive racing.

Other boards

Although most sailboards fall into one of the categories mentioned earlier, there are a few boards which are different in design or construction. As a rule these are either specially manufactured to meet a specific requirement or are designed for use in certain local conditions. Such boards are fairly unique and specialised and have no place in a general book on sailboarding such as this.

Class boards

In order to provide international competition, some sailboards are classified by the IYRU (International Yacht Racing Union). Such boards can engage in national or international class racing, the highest category of which is the Olympic Games. Typical of the recognised international classes are the 'Windsurfer' and 'Windglider', the

Wave boards provide the ultimate thrills. >

former and current sailboards respectively used for Olympic competition.

A class sailboard is built to strictly controlled specifications and its sail cut by a specified computer programme to ensure that it is exactly the same in all respects to other boards in the class. In this way no board can gain even the slightest advantage over another from either its construction or its rig. Since under these circumstances every sailboard is absolutely identical, the only difference between competitors is the skill of the riders.

Construction of a standard sailboard

A sailboard can be constructed from a number of materials, but the most common is a polyethylene

skin around a polyurethane foam core. Some other materials are occasionally used to form a skin instead of polyethylene. Fibreglass makes a light, strong skin but is easily damaged. A dent or crack in a fibreglass skin must be repaired immediately or water will seep into the foam core.

A polyethylene skin is more resilient and less likely to damage, although, of course, nothing is maintenance free, and a hard-used board, no matter what its construction, will need attention, even repair, from time to time. Exposure to wind and weather will not damage polyethylene to any great extent, but it can be weakened by long exposure to sunlight. For this reason a cover is a wise investment if your board is to be left out in the sunlight for long periods of time.

Most standard boards weigh in at around 18 kilograms with an overall length of around 3.5 metres and a width of 0.7 metres. A daggerboard slot is constructed on the centreline of the board into which the board is inserted either as a permanent fixture or when you are sailing. More detail about daggerboards or centreboards, as they are sometimes called, is given in the next section. The slot should be lined or fitted with a 'cassette' to protect the edges and prevent the skin splitting around the edges of the slot. Such damage frequently occurs when the board is run hard aground or is consistently sailed in shallow water.

All sailboards have the bow or nose turned up slightly to help them ride over small waves, or 'chop'. Some types of boards have their bows turned up more than others. Waveboards, for example, are well turned up to give them better lift over big waves and prevent the bow from nosing in to the crest. The bow of most boards can be turned up even more if required by covering the fore part with black material and weighing down heavily on the bow while applying modest heat. This procedure is known as 'scooping'.

A sailboard must be fitted with one or more skegs at its stern to give it good directional stability. This is particularly important when surfing down the face of a wave, so wave-riding boards often have two or three skegs, much the same as the skegs fitted to surfboards. Standard sailboards

Factory made boards are built under controlled conditions.

Scooping is mainly for wave boards. Flat boards go faster.

usually have only one skeg which is screwed into a recess in the board for easy removal and replacement if it breaks. Skegs vary enormously in shape according to the type of board to which they are secured, and the job it has to do.

All sailboards have non-skid surfaces on their upper deck to provide good foot grip when sailing. However, this surface is often not adequate when wet and the board is sailing hard, so some form of foot gear with suitable non-skid soles may be necessary in these conditions. Wave-jumping boards and some high performance boards have footstraps fitted into the deck to provide a firm grip and good foot control of the board when in action.

The daggerboard

The daggerboard is as important a part of the sailboard's equipment as the sails. Without it the board could only sail downwind. Any attempt to sail across or into the wind would result in the board going sideways. The full effect of the daggerboard and the principle behind its use are described in more detail in Chapter 3.

Basically, the daggerboard prevents the sailboard slipping sideways across the water as a result of the pressure of wind on the sails. It presents a surface which resists sideways movement through the water but permits forward movement. It has its greatest effect on the perfor-

Without the daggerboard, the board would skid sideways across the water.

extent, but as the wind comes round to the beam (90 degrees to the bow) it is partly raised. When the wind is right astern and no sideways pressure is experienced, the daggerboard is raised totally or removed from its slot.

There is a variety of daggerboards available, the simplest being a roughly rectangular-shaped board with a cap which is inserted in the daggerboard slot and raised or lowered by hand to the required position. More sophisticated daggerboards are fitted permanently into the board and are operated by foot. These swing down beneath the board and retract back up into a recess in the bottom.

Daggerboards also vary in size and shape according to the wind conditions in which they are used, although as a general rule, such sophisticated equipment is confined to high-performance racing. The shape of the daggerboard affects the board's performance, and maintaining good performance through strong winds requires a different shape of daggerboard to normal wind conditions. Freestyle performance may also demand a more sophisticated daggerboard than that used for everyday sailing.

The mast

Most sailboard masts are made of extruded aluminium tubing or fibreglass and are tapered towards the top. To absorb the stress of the wind filling the sail, the mast must be very flexible, and to prevent it filling with water it must be securely plugged at both ends. A standard sailboard mast is about 4.2 metres long and is secured at the bottom end to a universal joint, which enables it to be turned in any direction. The universal joint is mounted onto a plug or some other fitting which enables it to be plugged firmly into a recess or hole in the sailboard.

The mast on a sailboard has much wider use than its counterpart on a conventional sailing boat. On the latter, its main purpose is to hold the sails in position to catch wind. On a sailboard it serves the same purpose but also acts as the steering device, for sailboards are not fitted with rudders. Unlike a yacht mast, the sailboard mast does not remain permanently vertical to the deck, but can be leaned in all directions to per-

mance of the board when the sideways wind pressure is greatest—that is when the wind is ahead or on the side. When the wind is blowing from behind, there is no sideways pressure and so the daggerboard is not required.

In practice, the greatest sideways pressure comes when the board is sailing into the wind. The more the wind angle increases, the less sideways factor is experienced and the less the need for the daggerboard. Thus when sailing to windward the daggerboard is lowered to its fullest form a variety of services. Hence the need for it to be mounted on a universal joint.

The sail is usually 'sleeved' onto the mast, an opening in the sleeve enabling the boom to be attached. A tension device termed the 'down-haul'—usually a light line or purchase between the bottom of the sail and an eye at the foot of the mast—ensures that the sail is fitted tightly along the length of the mast, a factor which can greatly affect the performance of the board.

The mast and boom are simply constructed but very effective in use.

The boom

The 'wishbone' boom is also used on some yachts, but has been developed considerably in the design of sailboards. It is made from extruded aluminium tubing with injected plastic or nylon mouldings plugged into the ends of the two tubes to secure them together. Some form of rubber or synthetic grip material covers the front sections of the boom tubes, for the bare aluminium is very slippery when wet and would create problems when sailing in any but very light winds.

The front end of the boom is secured to the mast by means of either a light line or some patent device which allows the boom to move easily, particularly in the horizontal plane. This is known as the 'inhaul'. A special hitch—usually a 'Prusik' hitch—is used to ensure that the boom does not slip up or down the mast although, as mentioned, some manufacturers use patent devices made of shock cord or similar material to secure their booms to the mast. The type of securing device is not important providing the boom is firmly attached.

The outer end of the boom is equipped with fittings to enable the back corner of the sail to be tensioned outwards from the mast by a line known as the 'outhaul'. Once again, this may take a variety of forms, although the most common consists of a light line reeved through holes in the end of the boom and secured to cleats on the boom arms. Adjustment of sail tension with the outhaul is important to the sailing performance of the board when wind conditions vary.

Another rope attached to the front end, or handle of the boom is the 'uphaul'. This is the rope used to raise the rig from the water. It is usually a rope of fairly good dimensions with knots tied at intervals to provide hand grips when the rope is wet and slippery. It is secured at the handle by a knot, and hangs down the front of the mast when upright, usually secured to the base of the mast by means of shock cord, known as a 'bungee', or a length of light line. The uphaul is never tensioned, but allowed to hang fairly loose, and if correctly secured should always be easily reached from the board. Without the shock cord securing it to the base of the mast, the uphaul will float off out of reach when the rig is in the water.

The sail

Sailboard sails are usually made of Dacron or Mylar—synthetic materials which have remarkable endurance considering the rough treatment they encounter. Sails are cut to different shapes and sizes to fit different boards and to provide different standards of performance in different sailing conditions. Standard sailboard sails are of quite different shape to wave-board sails. And heavy weather sails are of different size and material to those used in light weather. The sailmaker's skill lies in shaping each sail to provide maximum performance under the conditions for which it is designed.

All sails are cut into an aerofoil shape, not unlike the shape of an aircraft wing. Indeed, the performance of a sail is very similar to that of a wing, as described in Chapter 3. To obtain this shape, the sailmaker sews together a series of curved panels of sailcloth (known as 'cloths') in such a manner that when full of wind the sail falls into an aerofoil shape. The sail then provides forward drive for the sailboard in just the same way a wing provides lift for an aircraft.

Once this aerofoil shape has been obtained, then the sail must be trimmed to suit the rig for which it is designed. Large sails of lightweight material catch a lot of wind and are therefore designed for light-weather performance. By contrast, strong winds demand not only smaller sail area, but also sails made from much stronger material. Beginners usually start with somewhat smaller sails than average so that they can master the techniques without the frustration of being forever pulled over into the water. Children, lacking the strength to pull up a standard rig, also need much smaller sails, often with smaller masts and booms.

All sails used for sailboarding are three cornered and their parts are named identically to those used for conventional sailcraft. The top corner is known as the 'peak', the corner secured to the outer end of the boom as the 'clew', and the corner at the bottom of the mast as the 'tack'. The front edge of the sail is called the 'luff' and the rear edge the 'leech', while the bottom edge is known as the 'foot'.

The peak of the sail is strengthened to form a cap over the end of the mast, and this is a perma-

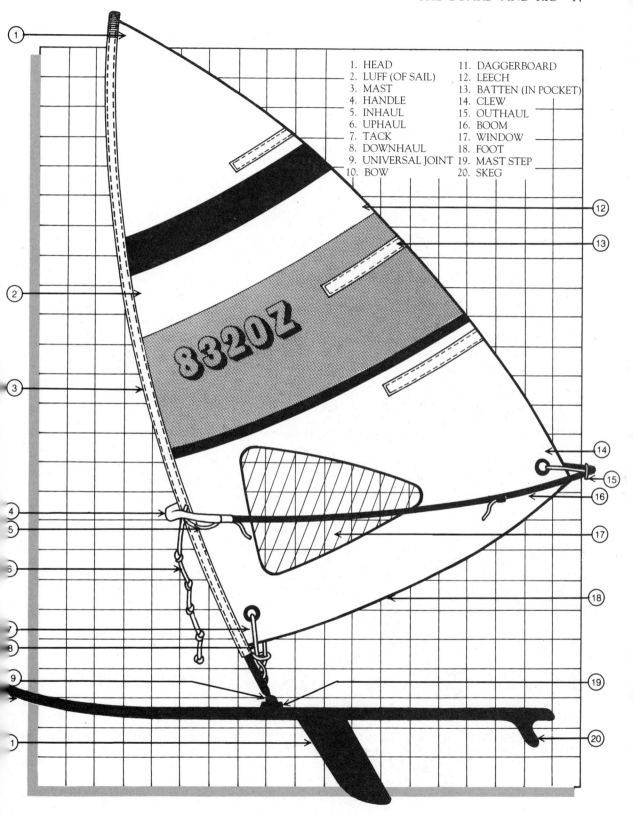

1. HEAD
2. LUFF (OF SAIL)
3. MAST
4. HANDLE
5. INHAUL
6. UPHAUL
7. TACK
8. DOWNHAUL
9. UNIVERSAL JOINT
10. BOW
11. DAGGERBOARD
12. LEECH
13. BATTEN (IN POCKET)
14. CLEW
15. OUTHAUL
16. BOOM
17. WINDOW
18. FOOT
19. MAST STEP
20. SKEG

nent fitting. But the other two corners have adjustable lines attached to them so that the luff and leech can be tensioned and thus the shape of the sail changed according to wind conditions. The line tensioning the clew to the end of the boom is known as the 'outhaul', and the line secured at the tack, which tensions the luff of the sail, is the 'downhaul'.

The aerofoil shape of the sail can be clearly seen here.

Standard-rig sails usually have an area of between 5.5 and 6.3 square metres, the average being somewhere around 5.8 square metres. Small sails for beginners are usually around 2.7 square metres in area, while storm sails used in winds over 20 knots are mostly in the range 3.7 to 5 square metres. Light-weather sails may be up to 9 square metres in area.

The profile of the sail will vary according to the rig it is attached to, the notable variations being between standard sailboard rigs and those used for wave-jumping. With wave-jumping boards, for example, the clew, or back corner of the sail is cut higher than normal in order to keep the sail out of the water when sheeting on to make a jump. High aspect ratio sails are narrower at the boom and taller up the mast. These are popular with some high performance sailors.

Windows are an important part of a sail for they allow the boardrider clear vision of anything approaching behind the sail. This is essential when sailing among other craft, and also when wave-jumping, for without a clear view of an approaching wave, the boardrider cannot pick the right spot to make his approach and subsequent jump. The size of the window is related not only to the view it offers, but also to the strength of the sail, for the clear plastic material stitched into the sail to provide the window is not as strong as the sailcloth and thus creates a weak area.

Battens are also an important part of the sail equipment for they help to shape the sail. While some learner rigs may not carry battens in their sails, most sails for standard sailboards have short battens. High performance and wave rigs often have full-width battens that fit right through the sail to retain the aerofoil section so vital to the sail's performance. As a rule, battens are made of nylon or plastic, although bamboo cane may also be used if the synthetic material is not available or is too expensive.

Some sails have sophisticated refinements such as leech lines which allow more shape to be induced into the sail to suit changing conditions. However, like most refinements, these are orientated around racing or specialised performance and are not normally found on standard boards.

Full width battens retain the sail shape under all conditions.

A similar refinement is a reefing sail. A zipper inserted in the sail enables a large area to be zippered off in order to reduce sail area for increasing wind strengths. This avoids the need to change sail when the wind increases in the course of a race.

2. Before Setting Out

Transporting the board

The sailboard must be transported to the water and that almost invariably means carrying it on the car roof. Special racks are available which take much of the hassle out of loading and unloading, as well as ensuring that the board fits snugly and is unlikely to move in transit. The extra expense involved in such a rack is well justified although, of course, the basic roof bars with foam rubber covering will do the job providing the board is well mounted and well lashed.

The board must be loaded onto the racks upside down, bow forward, and with the boom and mast lashed on top or to one side of it. Once again, specially made racks often have recesses to cater for boom and mast which fit snugly underneath or to one side of the board and are automatically locked in place when the board is strapped down. Special quick release straps are handy although if the journey to the water is a short one, shock or bungy cord will do the trick. If any part of the mast hangs over the back of the car—which it almost inevitably will—then a red rag may be required, to conform with road rules.

Although more energetic sailboarders may lift a sailboard onto the racks from the side of the car without any effort, and this is particularly the case with small wave-jumping boards, the easiest way is to rest the bow of the board on the rear rack and slide it forward from behind the car until in position on both racks. It is a good idea when loading a board and rig, to let them drain in the near vertical position for a few minutes before loading, as water, particularly salt water, which may be trapped in the gear will later drain out all over the car bodywork and possibly cause rust spots.

Carrying the gear

From the car to the water may be quite a step, and will probably require two journeys to transfer all the gear. The board is the heaviest item, and for ease of carrying is best held with the top deck against your hip and your fingers inserted into the daggerboard slot from the outside. If the board has a permanently fitted daggerboard then it will be necessary to adjust your grip. Once on the beach, or the water's edge, the board must be placed top down to avoid damage to the skeg.

Rigging

With all the gear laid out on the beach, commence rigging as follows.

1. Thread the mast into the sail sleeve until it fits snugly along its full length. Thread the down-haul through the eye at the foot of the mast

The easiest way to carry a board.

and tension the sail firmly before securing the downhaul with two half hitches.

2. Thread the mast and sail through the boom until the boom is in its correct location with the handle level with the gap in the sail sleeve and the uphaul hanging down towards the foot of the mast. Then tilt the end of the boom upwards until the boom is aligned with the mast, but the handle is still in position at the gap in the sail sleeve.

3. Secure the boom to the mast using a Prusik hitch or whatever means is provided. In most designs the Prusik hitch is made around the mast where it is accessible through the gap in the sail sleeve. The free end of this hitch becomes the inhaul, which is threaded through holes in the handle to secure the boom firmly to the mast.

4. Bring the boom back to its normal position at right angles to the mast. Thread the outhaul

The board must be snugly loaded and well strapped down.

through the holes in the end of the boom, back through the clew of the sail and through the end of the boom again. Use this purchase to tension the sail as hard as possible, then secure the outhaul in the cleats provided on the boom.

5. Attach the shock cord of the uphaul either to the downhaul or to an eye provided at the foot of the mast. Do not tension this rope too much.

6. Insert the battens in their correct pockets. The rig is now ready to mount on the board.

Once rigging has been completed, carrying the rig down to the water can be quite a problem, particularly if there is any sort of a breeze blowing. Unless you carry it properly, you will risk cartwheeling down the beach or taking off like a

Rigging the sails

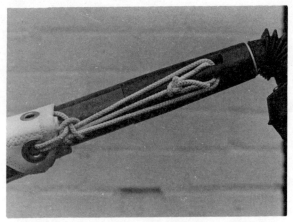

1. The downhaul tensions the sail downwards to the foot of the mast.

2. A Prusik hitch around the mast provides a securing point for the boom.

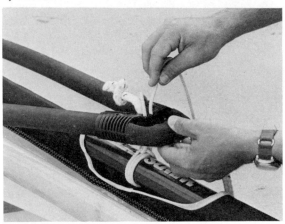

3. With the boom tilted, the inhaul is secured.

4. With the boom returned to its normal position, the outhaul is threaded through the clew of the sail.

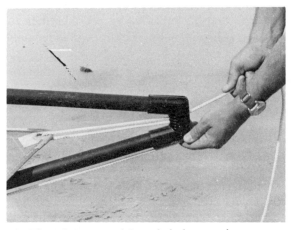

5. The sail is tensioned through the boom ends.

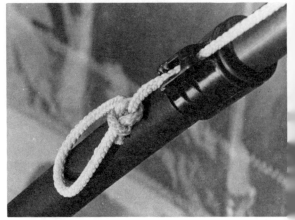

6. A cleat on the boom holds the outhaul in place. The knot is for added security.

hang-glider, for the wind in the sail creates just as powerful a force on land as it does on the water.

The correct way to carry the rig is with the mast, and thus the leading edge of the sail, above your head, directly across wind and facing into the wind. In this way, there will be a tendency for the sail to lift and fly, just like a hang-glider wing, but because it is not secured at the back end, the wind will spill before it creates any power or lift. This may mean walking sideways down the beach like an aerodynamic crab, but any tendency to turn the sail out of the wind will cause it to flip over and cartwheel; a performance which may not only be embarrassing, but also dangerous.

Launching

The rig should not be mounted on the board while it is still on the beach, or once again, it may catch a gust of wind and take off. The rig should be carried to the water's edge and thrown out into the water a few metres from the beach. The board can then be turned over and launched and pushed out to where the rig is floating. The final stages of rigging should take place in the water so that the board and rig can be kept under control.

The mast step is plugged into its socket, the daggerboard dropped into its slot, and the board is ready to sail. While everything is lying in the water it will remain placid so now is the time to make any final adjustments. If a safety line is fitted to the base of the mast, it should be connected to its fitting on the board at this stage. This will prevent board and rig becoming separated after a spill. The daggerboard should not be fully lowered while close to the beach or it may dig into the bottom and snap off. Similarly, the board must be kept in at least knee-deep water to prevent damage to the skeg.

If you are not an experienced sailor, it is a good idea to paddle the board and rig out a few metres from the beach before making any attempt to sail, otherwise you may endanger swimmers. You will probably drop the mast a dozen times before getting your balance, and even when the mast is up, the board will tend to career around wildly until you get it under control. A dropped mast or a runaway board can give a swimmer a nasty crack on the head, so do your practising in deep water, away from the beach.

Clothing

Sailboarders are very susceptible to two health hazards, both of which are related to exposure to the elements. The first, and most obvious, is over-exposure to ultra-violet radiation from the sun. In temperate and warm climates the temptation is to sail with only light clothing such as board shorts, leaving most of the surface of the body exposed to sunlight. In small doses this is fine, but as you race across the waves, caught up in the exhilaration of the moment, you easily lose track of time, and before you even give it serious thought, the damage is done. Sunburn is both painful and a severe health risk and will at least inhibit your sailboarding in the following days. At worst it can land you in hospital with melanoma, a form of skin cancer that can be terminal.

You should always wear at least a T-shirt with your board shorts. Even then, your arms, thighs and face are exposed, and the radiation on the water is far greater than it is on the land. Melanoma in the thigh region is common, so take care not to over expose this area, and the forehead is a prime target for skin cancer in later life, so protect this area too. Blocking creams can take the place of clothing in some areas, for wearing too much gear can be very restricting in the active sport of sailboarding. On a sunny day you should never wear less than a hat (tied on), a T shirt and board shorts (almost down to the knees), using blockout cream on other exposed areas.

The second problem relates to over-exposure to cold rather than sunshine, and is therefore more orientated to colder climates, although it can easily occur even in tropical climates under certain conditions. Hypothermia is a condition in which the body loses heat to the point where the funtion of essential organs such as the heart is affected, and death can result. To most sailboarders it may sound a remote risk, but in fact hypothermia can strike very quickly and accounts for far more water-related deaths than does drowning.

A typical case might occur on a fine summer day with a moderate, cool, offshore breeze providing ideal conditions for sailboarding. A fairly inexperienced sailor launches his board off the beach for an hour's indulgence in close inshore waters. He is wearing a light T-shirt and shorts.

The wind gets up and in the exhilaration of a good sail, our boardrider gets farther offshore than he intended. When he turns to come home something goes wrong and he can make no progress back towards the shore. Despite following all the emergency procedures, he finds himself stuck out in open water with the wind beginning to bite through his saturated clothing. Within an hour this boardrider may develop hypothermia and subsequently die.

The cooling wind flowing over the surface of his wet skin acts in the same way as cool air in a

A short boardsuit is ideal for moderate weather. >

Final adjustments can be made in the water.

refrigerator. To prevent this action, some form of insulation is necessary and without doubt the best form of insulated clothing for sailboarding is the neoprene foam rubber wetsuits also used for surfing and skindiving. If the air is cool or there is a chance that it will get cool, or if you plan to sail for some length of time, you would be wise to don a wetsuit before stepping onto your board. Wetsuits designed for sailboarding usually have zippers so they can be opened if it gets too hot and for that matter you could take the jacket off and tie it round your waist if you find it cumbersome. But if the weather turns or you get stuck offshore, your life may depend on having a wetsuit with you, so it is a wise investment to wear one for all but local, inshore sailing in warm, stable conditions.

Only experts carry the rig like this!

If you cannot afford a wetsuit, then a woollen jumper is the next best thing. Any article of clothing that cuts the wind is better than nothing, but clothing that holds a layer of water is best. Water is a good insulator and a layer of water next to the skin keeps body heat in. It is on this principle that the wetsuit is designed, for the sponge material fills with water and creates an insulating layer around the body.

Although shoes will do little to retain body warmth, they are an important part of sailboarding gear, for many boards have poor non-skid surfaces on their decks, and when the wind gets up and you are flying along with everything drawing taught and terrific, nothing is more disconcerting than to have your feet keep slipping off the board. It invariably leads to a spill, and is wear one all the time. A tight-fitting lifejacket can be a good insulator and thus an important part of your clothing if the temperature is low. Special lifejackets made for sailboarding provide good buoyancy in the water but are compact and comfortable when sailing. Some are fitted with a back-pack and harness hook.

A back-pack can be useful if you are setting out on a lengthy sail. In it you can carry spare clothing, sun cream, even lunch if necessary, and a small back-pack will not hinder your sailing ability. Make sure, however, that everything in the pack is waterproof for if you spill, and you will almost certainly spill at some time, most back-packs will not prevent the contents from getting wet.

Weather

Nothing can change more quickly than the weather, and nothing is more likely to cause danger to a sailboarder than a sudden change in the weather. Apart from the risk of hypothermia mentioned in the previous section, a change of

The 'naked' sailboarder is inviting trouble.

Sensible clothing for cool conditions - wetsuit and lifejacket.

frustrating and annoying when everything else is going well. A pair of neoprene foam bootees or even a pair of sandshoes with good tread on the soles will give a firm footing and enable you to stretch the board to its limit without it suddenly shooting out from under your feet.

The question of lifejackets is usually controlled by the maritime authorities. It may be compulsory to wear a lifejacket or it may not. Either way, it goes without saying that wearing a lifejacket is a wise procedure for all but close-inshore sailing, and if you are not a strong swimmer, you should

Sailboarders' delight—a stiff sea breeze.

weather can bring up winds which will make the board unmanageable, perhaps unsailable, and blow you out into danger before you have time to put into effect emergency procedures. It may bring up choppy seas which, to the uninitiated can also make it difficult to handle the board and sail back to safety.

The biggest danger to novices is that of being blown out to sea by an unexpected offshore wind. A sudden shift in direction and increase in wind strength such as comes with weather changes like cold fronts, can create problems even for the relatively experienced sailboarder. It can create considerable danger for the inexperienced.

Learning a little about the weather is a good idea, or failing that, at least learn to read the daily weather chart published in newspapers or screened on TV. Fronts and similar severe weather changes are easily recognised, as are changes in wind direction and strength in the normal movement of weather patterns. In many coastal waters the sea breeze plays a predominant role, and it is important to know that the sea breeze will increase as the land gets hotter during a normal summer's day. Most important of all, check the official weather forecast before you set off to the beach so that if there is a change coming through, you will have some idea of when it will arrive. A phone call takes only a moment of time and can avoid a very unpleasant experience later in the day.

3. How It All Works

The theory of sailing

You just need to stand near a busy highway to appreciate that anything moving at speed creates a suction effect. Big trucks roaring by tend to draw you into their wake with the suction created by their speed. Another example is the suction action of 'venturi' balers fitted to fast boats. This type of baler consists basically of a hole in the bottom of the boat. When the boat is moving fast, the speed of the water travelling past this hole sucks out any water in the boat and thus keeps the inside of the hull dry. Of course, the minute the boat stops, unless the hole is stoppered, the outside water will pour in, for the suction effect of the hull speed is lost.

These examples illustrate the basic principle behind the working of a sail. A sail is cut into a curved shape so that wind travelling around the outside of the curve is speeded up and flows faster than the wind travelling around the inside of the sail. The faster wind on the outside of the curve creates a suction which draws the sail towards it thus creating a movement which is transferred to the board and causes it to travel through the water.

The special curve cut into the sail is called an 'aerofoil' shape because it is similar in cross-section to the shape of an aircraft wing. The same principle applies to the surface of a wing, but in this case, since the outside of the curve (with the suction effect) is on the top, the wing tends to be sucked upwards as the aircraft gathers speed, thus lifting it into the air.

Forward movement

The theoretical point at which the suction effect works on a sail is known as the 'Centre of Effort' (CE). If the wind is coming from behind and you want to sail straight downwind, then all the forces are working to draw the sail straight ahead so there is no problem. But if the wind is coming from the side, then some of the force working through the CE is tending to draw the board sideways. Since no-one wants to sail sideways, some means has to be used to convert this sideways movement into forward movement.

This is done with the daggerboard. Without the daggerboard the sailboard would simply skid sideways across the water. Lowering the daggerboard creates a resistance to sideways movement because the daggerboard is wide and flat. It creates resistance to sideways movement but allows forward movement. This resistance is

The wind, travelling faster round the outside of the curved sail, creates a vortex which pulls the board along.

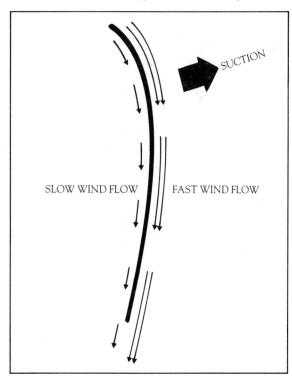

SUCTION

SLOW WIND FLOW   FAST WIND FLOW

focussed around a point on the daggerboard known as the 'Centre of Lateral Resistance' (CLR).

Just as an orange pip squeezed between thumb and finger must fly forwards, so the sailboard, squeezed between the pressures of wind through the CE and the opposing pressures of water through the CLR, has nowhere to go but forwards.

Steering

If the board is to go straight ahead, then obviously the pressures on the CE and CLR must be equal and acting against one another on the same

The wind pressure through the CE, and the water resistance, through the CLR, 'squeeze' the board forward.   >

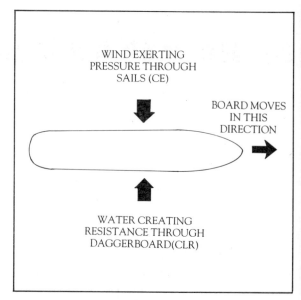

WIND EXERTING
PRESSURE THROUGH
SAILS (CE)

BOARD MOVES
IN THIS
DIRECTION

WATER CREATING
RESISTANCE THROUGH
DAGGERBOARD(CLR)

of the CLR. The pressure on the sail will push the bow of the board away from the wind, and the water pressure on the daggerboard will accentuate this. A twisting action will be set up which will cause the board to turn away from the wind. Similarly, if the CE is moved behind the CLR the board will turn into the wind.

The daggerboard is a permanent fixture and so the CLR cannot be moved, but by means of the

Wind ahead, sail in tight.

Mast back, board rounds up into the wind.

theoretical spot. Since one is above the water and one below, they cannot act on the same spot, but providing they are on the same vertical line the effect is the same. If, however, one centre of pressure is ahead or astern of the other they will have a twisting effect on the board which will cause it to turn rather than move ahead in a straight line. It is this factor which permits the board to be steered.

If we start with the CE and CLR acting directly on the same vertical line, the board will move straight forward. Now let's move the CE forward

Mast forward, board turns away from the wind.

universal joint the sail can be moved in any direction. To steer the sailboard, then, the mast needs only to be moved forwards or backwards in order to move the CE of the sail ahead of, or behind the CLR. Leaning the mast forward takes the CE of the sail forwards of the CLR and causes the sailboard to sheer away from the wind. Leaning the mast back brings the CE behind the CLR and causes the board to round up into the wind. This is the basic principle of steering a sailboard.

Wind astern, sail run out.

The sailing positions

Having seen how the combination of sail and daggerboard can drive a sailboard in many directions, we now look at the limitations of this system. It is obvious that the aerofoil shape of the sail can only work effectively when the wind is at the correct angle to create a suction flow across its surface. And yet, if we are to manoeuvre our sailboard in all directions, this angle between wind and sail must change. This is overcome and the correct angle maintained by altering the position of the sail each time there is a change in the angle of the wind. In other words, each time the board changes direction and thus changes the angle between the wind and the sail, the sail must be repositioned to resume its original angle to the wind.

In practice, the correct angle between wind and sail is achieved as follows.

1. When the wind is ahead (or as nearly ahead as is possible), the sail is pulled tight in to the centreline of the board.
2. When the wind is right behind, the sail is run out until it is square to the centreline of the board.
3. Between these two extremes the sail is adjusted according to the wind direction. When the wind is on the beam, for example, halfway from ahead and astern, the sail is let out about halfway. The more the wind moves towards the stern the further the sail is let out, the closer the angle of the wind to the bow the more the sail is pulled in.

The principle sailing positions described above are given names as follows.

1. 'Close hauled'. Sailing as close to the wind as possible with the sail pulled tight in to the board.
2. 'Running free'. Sailing with the wind behind and the sail let out until it is at right angles to the board.
3. 'Reaching'. Sailing with the wind on the side somewhere between close hauled and running free.

angle is best determined visually by watching the front edge or 'luff' of the sail. A practical exercise will illustrate this:

Pull the sail tight into the board as for sailing close hauled, then bring the board slowly up into the wind. When the front edge of the sail begins to flutter—a condition known as 'luffing'—the board is sailing too close to the wind and must be turned back out of the wind until this luffing has stopped. The board is then sailing as close to the wind as possible.

< Wind on the beam, sail half out.

This luffing sail will soon reduce the board's speed.

Luffing

Maintaining the correct angle of the wind to the sail ensures a flow of air over the sail surface which will create the suction or 'drive', as it is termed, to move the board through the water. If the sail is not adjusted to maintain this angle one of two things will happen.

If the angle between sail and wind becomes too great (i.e. the board is reaching or running but the sails are kept in tight), the drive will be destroyed and the board will come to a stop.

If the angle becomes to narrow (i.e. the wind gets round the front of the sail), the sail will collapse and lose its aerofoil shape.

It is obviously important to know the narrowest angle the board can sail into the wind before the sail collapses. As a general rule it is around 50 degrees, but every sail is different and the exact

The non-sailing zone

Knowing just how close the board can sail to the wind is important in all types of sailing. Our destination may lie right in the eye of the wind, and since there is no way our board, or any other sailcraft for that matter, can sail directly into the wind, we must sail at the closest possible angle to the wind to get as close as possible to our destination.

As mentioned, this is probably about 50 degrees to the direction the wind comes from, so as we sail off close hauled and with the wind, say, on our left or port side, we will be 50 degrees off course. If we turn the board and sail close hauled with the wind on the other side, we will be 50 degrees off course on that side, too. So it means that there is a zone of 50 degrees on either side of the wind—100 degrees in all—in which our board cannot sail. This is known as the 'non-sailing zone' and no board can sail within that zone.

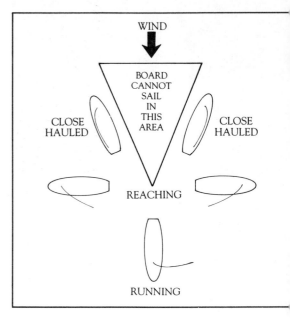

The non-sailing zone.

Port tack.

Beating or Tacking

Since we must be able to sail to any destination, even one which is directly in the eye of the wind, there must be a method of sailing to windward, even if it cannot be done directly. This is termed 'beating' or 'tacking' because the board is sailed first with the wind on one side and then with the wind on the other. To avoid confusion with another form of tacking which we encounter later, the term 'beating' is mostly used to describe progression into the wind.

Sailing with the wind on the left or port side, the board is said to be on a 'port tack'.

Sailing with the wind on the right or starboard side, the board is said to be on a 'starboard tack'.

To reach a windward destination the board is set up close hauled on one tack, sailed for a while then turned onto the other tack. The procedure is repeated so that the board makes a zig-zag course into the wind and across the non-sailing zone until the destination is reached. The exact distance sailed on each tack varies. In theory, if you sail long enough on the first tack until the

Starboard tack.

In irons

Getting the board from one tack to another involves sailing through the non-sailing zone, during which time the sail will luff and then collapse. The procedure for tacking across the wind is described later, but in theory it amounts to deliberately putting the board into the non-sailing zone and allowing its momentum to carry it across the other side. The speed of the board as it is swung up into the tack will determine whether it gets through, for when the sail collapses it loses all its drive, and only the board's momentum will carry it across to the other tack. If there is insufficient momentum, the board will stall and stop in the non-sailing zone.

The nautical term for this is 'in irons' or 'in stays', but it is often referred to simply as 'stalling'. When the board is caught in irons, there is nothing you can do but try to 'walk' her out of the non-sailing zone by using your feet and body to twist the board around.

destination is at an angle of 100 degrees to the bow, then the next tack will carry the board directly to the destination. However, this may involve going a long way out on one tack, so as a rule a series of short tacks is usually preferred. This aspect of beating is discussed in more detail in Chapter 4.

Beating to windward. In the forground a board tacks from port to starboard. In the background are boards on both port and starboard tacks.

4. Getting Started

Sailboarding is not difficult to learn. In the first instance you need only a few lessons to learn the basic skills, and the rest comes with practice. Of course as you improve on those basic skills you will need further tuition, but in the early days, practice, practice and more practice is the way to master sailboarding. While this applies to most sports, it applies particularly to sailboarding because the greatest single factor involved is balance, and balance only comes with practice. Once you have mastered balance, everything else comes fairly easily.

Try standing at first. Pulling up the rig can come later.

Balance

First steps in learning to handle a sailboard, then, revolve around getting your balance and the feel of the board under your feet. This should be done before even attempting to lift the sail from the water and certainly before allowing the sail to fill with wind. Initially it is hard enough to stand on or move around the board without having to handle a clumsy rig. If you attempt to start sailing without being totally relaxed and at ease in the standing position, you will be destined for many frustrating falls.

Leave the rig on the beach for the time being.

Just use the board on its own. Practise the follow-ing exercises. Go over each step time and again until you feel totally confident that you have your balance and are ready for the next step.

1. Push the board out a few metres from the beach, manoeuvre it so that it lies across the wind, and climb aboard.

2. Stand upright until you feel comfortable, then move slightly forwards and backwards, getting the feel of the board moving beneath your feet.

3. When you feel you are balancing comfortably, place one foot in front of the mast recess and one behind the daggerboard slot, with both feet on the centreline of the board and your body facing away from the wind. This is the basic starting position.

4. Get the feel of this position, then lean forward until you can touch the water. Lean backwards as well. These will be the actions you will use when pulling the rig out of the water. You need to be totally confident about them.

5. Stand upright in the starting position then move slowly forward around the mast recess until you are in the same position on the opposite side. This is the basic manoeuvre for changing tack. You will be doing it a lot when you start sailing.

6. Now start to turn the board with your feet. This will take a little practice but is important when sailing. The knack is to twist your body, using your legs as levers to move the board. Once you have gained your balance, your confidence and the ability to turn the board with your feet, you are ready to start sailing.

The starting position

The most important of all the basic steps, the starting position will be used every time you begin to sail and every time you spill. Until you master this step you will spend many frustrating hours trying to sail with no results other than frequent duckings! Without perfecting the start-ing position you have no chance of getting sailing other than perhaps by flying across the water totally out of control and with arms and legs

Don't be discouraged by a few falls. It will come eventually.

Balancing on the board takes some practice.

Even with the rig up, be very relaxed and just stand and stare....

1. Mast to leeward, daggerboard in, board across the wind.

2. Lean back on the uphaul, feet braced, back straight.

3. As the mast comes up, let it flap, lean back and relax.

4. This is the starting position.

flailing in all directions. Whenever you have a spill you come back to the basic starting position, so it is best to learn it well at the beginning and avoid hassle and frustration later.

With the board and rig in the water, well clear of swimmers, the procedure is as follows.

1. Plug the mast into its socket, making sure that the rig is on the opposite side of the board to the wind. Lower the daggerboard then stand up with your feet in the starting position on either side of the mast as described above.

2. Reach down and pick up the uphaul. This will give you something to hang on to. Now use your feet to turn the board until it is across wind, with your back to the wind. Get comfortable in this position.

Getting under way

1. *Keep the sail free until you are ready.*

2. *With the back hand holding the uphaul prepare to cross over hands to grip the boom.*

3. Make sure you are totally relaxed, for muscle tension will hinder smooth action, and smooth action is essential at this stage. Shake your arms and legs to ensure that they are relaxed and free.

4. Keeping your back straight (this is most important), bend your knees until you are in a squatting position, then take up the slack of the uphaul.

5. Keeping tension on the uphaul, slowly straighten your knees, keeping your back straight. As you rise, the rig will rise out of the water with you. It will be heavy at first, so rise slowly to allow the water in the sail to drain out. Once it is out of the water move your hands up the uphaul until you are in the full standing position, holding the rig by the top of the uphaul.

6. Get comfortable in this position, leaning back a little if needs be to counterbalance the rig, which should be idly flapping as you hold it by the top of the uphaul. If the board has moved out of position, use your feet to get it back until it is lying across wind. You are now in the starting position.

Getting under way

Once you are comfortable in the starting position and feel you have confidence and control of the board, it is time to get under way. Once again total relaxation is important, for tensed muscles and nerves never perform fluently and you will find that you are either moving jerkily or over-reacting to unexpected developments, both of which will lead quickly to your first spill. Stay for some time in the starting position until you feel totally balanced and relaxed and ready to move slowly and easily on to the next stage.

3. Tilt the mast forward, sheet on slowly with the back hand.

4. As the weight comes on the boom, lean back.

1. Determine which will be your front and back hands when you begin to sail. The front hand will be the one nearest the mast and its main purpose will be to hold the mast upright or lean it in any required direction. The back hand will grip well along the boom and adjust the sail for the wind direction and strength. Bringing the sail in towards the board is called 'sheeting in', and letting it run out is called 'easing away'.

2. If it is not already there, transfer the uphaul into the back hand. Cross over hands and grasp the boom a few centimetres back from the handle with the front hand.

3. Release the uphaul, holding the rig with the front hand, and place the back hand on the boom a comfortable distance behind the front hand.

4. Tilt the mast forward towards the bow a little and at the same time sheet in by pulling the

boom in with the back hand. This will cause the board to turn off the wind and fill the sail. Lean back to counter the increasing pressure of the rig.

5. As the board begins to move forward, bring the mast back to the vertical and sheet in with the back hand sufficiently to correct any luffing that may appear along the front edge of the sail.

Controlling the board

With the board moving ahead, it is important to control it fully. This is done in two ways—by steering with the sail and by adjusting the back hand to counter varying pressures of wind on the sail.

Turning the board is a combination of tilting the mast and sheeting in or out. The mast is tilted forward and the sail eased out to turn the board

Controlling the board

1. Tilting the mast forward turns the board away from the wind.

2. Tilting the mast back rounds the board up into the wind.

away from the wind. The mast is tilted back and the sail sheeted in to turn the board into the wind.

Adjusting for wind strength merely means easing away with the back hand to spill wind each time the rig becomes excessively heavy, or sheeting on if the sail begins to luff. As the board starts to move and you sheet in, you will feel the rig pull you forward and upset your balance. At first you can counter this by leaning back to the point where, ideally, you are hanging out over the water. But if the wind strengthens and you are still being pulled forward, you will need to spill wind by easing away the back hand and letting the sail luff a little.

As you gain confidence and the board begins moving faster, start to experiment with simple manoeuvres such as the following.

1. While sailing along, tilt the mast forward and ease away with the back hand. Push down with your front foot. The board will turn away from the wind. As the board begins to reach and then run before the wind you will find your feet automatically moving back along the board and taking up a position with one foot on either side of the centreline, in order to retain balance.

2. Tilt the mast back and sheet in with the back hand, at the same time pushing down with your back foot. The board will turn up into the wind. Be careful not to turn too far or you will run up into the non-sailing zone and the board will stall in irons.

3. With the wind right astern and the boom out at right angles, steering is best done by tilting the rig to the opposite side you want the board to turn, and assisting the turn by twisting with your feet. Steering is always less responsive when running than when in other sailing positions.

3. With the wind astern the sail is brought across the board.

4. The feet play an important part in steering.

Tacking

1. Close hauled to starboard, preparing to tack.

2. Mast back, move up to the mast.

Tacking

Tacking, or 'going-about', is the action of changing the wind from one side to the other by steering into and across the wind. Since it means passing through the non-sailing zone, the board must be moving fast with plenty of momentum if it is to avoid stalling in that zone. The procedure is as follows.

1. Assuming you are in a reaching position, then tilt the mast back, sheet in hard and race the board up into the wind. Place your front hand on the mast.

2. As the sail begins to luff, tilt the mast back more, and push down hard with your back foot.

3. Release you back hand and start to walk round the mast, helping the board to turn with your feet. Grasp the mast or handle with what was the back hand (it will now become the front hand).

4. Take the weight of the rig with this hand, releasing the old front hand as you continue to walk round the mast.

5. When the board is right round and the wind is on the other side, move your hands to take up the normal sailing grip on the boom, tilt the mast forward, sheet in with the new back hand and commence sailing on the other tack.

3. *Change grip, grab the opposite boom.*   4. *Mast forward, sheet on, lean back.*

Gybing

1. *Running free to starboard.*

2. *Gybe-oh, the sail swings across the bow.*

3. *Sheet on, lean back, running free to port.*

Gybing

It is also possible to change tack when running free with the wind behind. This manoeuvre is called 'gybing' and is much easier than tacking for it does not involve turning the board into the wind nor crossing the non-sailing zone. It is carried out as follows.

1. Because the board is running before the wind, the sail will be set out at right angles. When you are ready to gybe, place the front hand on the handle and release the back hand.

2. The boom and sail will swing forward and across the bow. Change hands on the handle, then reach forward with your free hand and grasp the boom as it swings around the other side.

3. Now the board is running free on the opposite tack and you simply adjust the position of your hands on the boom for normal sailing.

Sailing around the compass

This is a favourite exercise with sailboard instructors for it puts together all the basic manoeuvres described above, and takes the board through every manoeuvre that will be encountered in normal sailing. The idea is to start close hauled and sail right around in a wide circle through 360 degrees, returning to the starting position. It is done first clockwise and then anti-clockwise.

1. With the board close hauled on (say) a port tack, turning around in a clockwise circle means first easing away to the reach and run positions. Tilt the mast forward, ease away on the back hand until the board is sailing across wind.

2. To get into the running position, tilt the mast forward more and start to swing it across the board, moving your feet backwards. Ease out the sail until it is at right angles to the centreline and your feet are on either side of the centreline. You are now running free on a port tack.

3. To continue the turn you must change tack, and changing tack with the wind astern means gybing. Swing the sail across as described earlier and take up your new position with the board running free on a starboard tack.

4. Now the board must be brought up to the close hauled position, and this is done by tilting the mast back and sheeting in the boom. Be careful not to over-shoot the close hauled position or the board will stall into the wind. Watch for the first signs of luffing.

5. With the board close hauled on a starboard tack, to get back to our starting position, we must go about or tack. Make sure the board has good speed to get through the non-sailing zone, tilt the mast right back and tack over to the close hauled port tack position.

6. With the board sailing close hauled to port, you have completed a circle, sailing through 360 degrees of the compass and utilising every basic manoeuvre in normal use.

7. Now try the same routine again, this time sailing anti-clockwise around the compass. These two exercises are excellent training vehicles and will add a polish to your performance very quickly.

1. *Easing away on a port tack.*

4. *Closing up on a starboard tack.*

2. *Running free on a port tack.*

3. *Gybe-oh,* onto the starboard tack.

5. *Ready to tack.*

6. *Lee-oh, and back to the port tack.*

Beating to windward

As described in the previous chapter, no board can sail directly into the wind and the closest angle most can sail is around 50 degrees to the wind. Thus to sail towards an objective that lies close to the wind, a procedure known as 'beating to windward' is employed. This involves sailing as close to the wind (close hauled) as possible, first on one tack and then the other. The procedure is as follows.

1. Sheet in the sail, keep the mast upright and sail the board in the close hauled position.

2. As you sail along, the wind may shift, so try every now and then to sail a little closer to the wind. The minute the sail luffs you have gone too close and must bear away again. Indeed, beating to windward involves constantly checking to see that you are sailing as close to the luffing position as possible without actually luffing, thus making the best possible progress into the wind.

3. Keep a careful watch on your destination. As you sail on the first leg you will get closer to it, albeit at an angle. The objective will appear to move from ahead, down the side of the board.

4. When it has well passed the beam (90 degrees to the centreline), make a tack. On the new leg your destination should appear almost right ahead. If you can sail directly to it, do so, but more than likely, because of sideways drift, you will need to make a couple more tacks to reach it.

5. This procedure is fine for short windward beating, but when the object is some distance away, sailing off until it is past the beam may involve sailing a long way out on the first leg. In this case it is better to take a series of shorter legs, merely tacking when you think you have gone far enough on one leg. As you gain experience, your instinct will tell you when is the best time to tack.

6. The system used when racing is to begin with fairly long tacks and reduce the length of the legs as you approach the destination, thus sailing inside a theoretical 'cone', the apex of which is the destination. Such a practice avoids the risk of being caught by a wind shift when way out on one leg and losing ground a competitor. The sides of this cone, which determine the limits of each leg are called 'lay lines'.

The Olympic course

This is the term given to a race course which has three legs, one of which is directly into the wind. It is standard practice for most courses and in particular, as its name denotes, for international competition. Such a course makes an excellent follow-up to sailing around the compass and develops your skills even further. While it involves the same basic sailing manoeuvres, it also incorporates tacking or beating to windward, probably the most testing of all sailboard activities.

To make your own Olympic course, just select three buoys or marks already in place, or drop three plastic bottles secured by a length of line to a weight. The three markers should be roughly in the form of a triangle, and one leg must be directly into the wind. Once you can sail proficiently and quickly around this course, you can consider yourself an accomplished sailboarder!

An Olympic course for sailboard races.

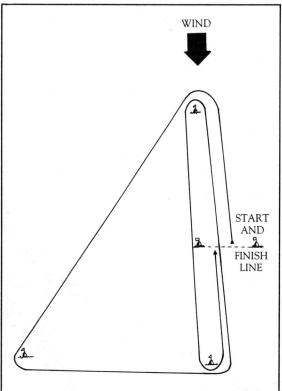

Beating to windward (lay lines).

The two boards on the right are on starboard tacks, the other two on port tacks. They are beating towards the far shore.

5. Sailing in Stronger Winds

At this stage in your sailboarding career, you should be handling winds of up to about 10 knots without too much problem, using the 'safety valve' of your sheeting hand to ease the sail and spill wind in stronger gusts or when the rig seems to be getting too heavy. As the wind picks up to 13-15 knots, however, you will find it necessary to change your techniques, because in that weight of breeze the standard techniques need some refining. You will find that when you spill wind with your sheeting hand, it is very hard to get the sail sheeted in again and the new force of the wind in the sail will tend to continually pull you forward and upset your balance.

Even getting the rig up out of the water can be a problem, for the board careers around like a mad thing, and the flogging sail, when you finally get it up, is totally unmanageable. Practising in gradually increasing wind strengths will adjust your techniques, of course, but that is not always possible. Mostly you go out on a day that is quite

Getting the rig up can be the hardest part.

a bit stronger than you have been used to, and find the board and rig has turned into a mad thing that totally shatters your newly found confidence.

However, do not despair, for every beginner goes through this stage. Moving from under 10 knots to over 10 knots of wind strength is a barrier that causes traumas for everyone. To overcome this barrier, the first and most important thing is to ensure that you are totally competent at handling the board in the lighter breezes. Complete familiarity with the rig and its idiosyncrasies, and confidence in handling it under all conditions up to 10 knots of wind speed are essential. Only when you have reached this stage will you be ready to tackle the 10-knot barrier with any degree of success.

Pulling up the rig

This is the first big hurdle to overcome in strong winds. Whereas to date you have lifted the rig slowly and steadily, if you do that in strong winds a gust will either tear it from your hands, or pull

Everything happens quicker in stronger winds.

you headlong into the sail. You must get it up quickly, and in particular get the end of the boom out of the water, for gusty winds shift direction quickly, and if the sail is halfway up and the clew is still in the water, the sail will fill with a bang and either pull you in the water or send you flying in all directions.

Getting the sail up quickly is not easy, for it is heavier than before and flogs madly as it comes up, throwing you off balance. But if you have perfected the technique in quieter winds it is only a further step to bend your knees even more, give a solid heave as you straighten them and get the sail up in one swift movement.

With the end of the boom in the water the sail is, in effect, sheeted on. It cannot fly free or flap and spill wind, so the pressure builds up in the sail and drives the board forward at speed, not only making it even harder to get the rig up, but also upsetting your balance. It is often best to take your first few windy days with a smaller sail, for not only will it give you less weight to drag out of the water, but being shorter along the foot, the clew will come up out of the water more quickly than that of a full-sized sail.

Once the rig comes up, it will flog madly in the stronger winds, but there will be little weight in it and providing you are well balanced on the board, you should be able to stand and hold it without too much trouble. However, when you start to sheet on, the sail will fill quickly and suddenly, and unless you are prepared it will send you cartwheeling over the top in one quick bang! Getting the sail up is one problem. Getting it filled and under control is another.

The secret is to bring the sail over your head as you sheet on, pulling it right over to the windward side of the board. By so doing you will reduce the area of sail facing the wind and thus reduce the pressure. As you get the board sailing, you pull the sail right down to the point where not only is there far less weight in the rig, but the board then comes under complete control.

This technique is the secret of strong wind sailing. Pulling the sail over the board to windward not only presents less surface area to the

The stronger the wind, the more the rig must be pulled over you.

Racing is great sport when the breeze is up.

wind, but presents an angled surface rather than a flat one. It is obvious that the wind, glancing off an angled surface, will be far less powerful than the same wind slamming straight into a flat, perpendicular surface.

Another problem in stronger winds is the tendency for the board to nose into the water. The greater pressure in the sail will push the nose down and it will perform a respectable imitation of a submarine unless you move back quickly to counter it. Whereas you should have your front foot in front of the mast step in normal wind strengths, in stronger winds you must move it back beside or even behind the mast step. This means adjusting your hands on the boom, for if you pull the mast back as you move back, the board will round up into the wind and you will lose control.

The following is a summary of the basic points for getting under way and sailing in strong winds.

1. Get yourself well braced on the board before attempting to lift the rig out of the water. Move your feet back somewhat from the normal starting position and bend your knees well, keeping your back straight. Any tendency to bend your back or lean forward will be disastrous.

2. Pull the rig out of the water as quickly as possible. Particularly, get the end of the boom out of the water.

3. Continue to pull the rig back over your head, leaning backwards with it and reaching up with your back hand to sheet on as soon as you feel yourself falling backwards. This is the most difficult part of the manoeuvre. If you sheet on too soon you will be pulled headlong over the lee side, and if you leave it too late you will fall backwards into the drink! It takes a lot of practice to become familiar with this starting procedure.

4. The moment the board starts to leap forward, move your feet back along the board, pull the sail down further over your head and push hard with your feet. The board should now come under control and you will begin to feel some confidence. While the technique of spilling wind by easing the sheet hand still applies, you will find that with practice you can reduce or increase the pressure in the sail by the amount you pull it down over you.

Strong winds and surf make exhilarating sailing.

1. *Everything ready, waiting for the right puff.*

2. *Foot up, mast up, push off.*

3. *Away we go!*

Standing start

Smaller boards such as waveboards can get away to a standing start without dropping the rig in the water. Some standard boards with storm rigs may also use this technique, although as a rule the rig on these boards is a little on the heavy side. It is worth trying, however, for it eliminates the really heavy part of getting the sail up out of the water, sheeting on and pulling the rig down to windward over your head.

The sail is actually pulled over to windward before you start: so far over to windward, in fact, that it has little or no weight and catches no wind. This is done in the shallows as you prepare to start, and with the board pushed out ahead and across the wind. You will initially find that the board will try to swivel around on the universal joint and must be pushed back into place with your foot or by forcing the mast to one side, while awaiting the right puff of wind to make a start. This is where standard boards give most trouble, for apart from the heavier rig, the bigger, heavier board is harder to control in these conditions.

With the board aligned across the wind and the rig pulled down over your head to windward and free to flap, watch for the right moment. A lull, or drop in the breeze will provide the opportunity to raise the sail a little until it catches the wind, then, as the wind picks up again and the pressure comes on, you step smartly onto the board, sheet on as it moves forward, and settle immediately into the strong wind sailing position. Done properly, this is an effective and impressive manoeuvre with the board sweeping quickly away from the beach and screaming off across the water. Since you are virtually already in position when you step onto the board, only minor adjustments of feet and hands should be necessary when the wind slams down at full strength again and the board takes off at high speed.

Tacking

This is a fairly easy manoeuvre in strong winds since the board has a natural tendency to round up, and you have the mast fairly well pulled back anyway. By pulling it down a little harder and pushing the board away with your back foot, you will force it quickly up into the wind. Now you need to be very nimble. As the pressure comes off the sail, let the rig stand upright, nip around the mast, changing hands as you go, and get ready on the other side to pull the rig hard over to windward the moment you start to sheet on. There is no great need for speed, of course, for with the board headed into wind and the sail flapping, you can take all the time in the world to get ready for the next tack. But swinging around in a flying tack is a technique that is relatively easy to master and looks very impressive. What is more, for some strange reason it seems more natural—and thus easier—to keep the board moving once you start the tacking manoeuvre.

Bearing away

Turning away from the wind (towards the running position) is the hardest manoeuvre in strong winds for the same reasons that tacking is relatively easy. The board has a natural tendency to pull up into the wind and will resist violently your attempts to turn the bow away. Also, leaning the mast forward tends to make it come upright, thus creating greater pressure in the sail as the wind comes behind. Unless you are very careful the sail will pull you forward off balance and you will go flying over the bow. Many an experienced board sailor has spent hours being catapulted over the bow trying to execute this manoeuvre!

The secret again lies in keeping the sail pulled down over your head. Instead of tilting the mast forward as you would in normal winds, swing it over towards the windward side, pushing hard with your front foot and pulling in with your back foot, to turn the bow away from the wind. If you let the rig come upright even a little it will whisk you over the top, so get almost into a squatting position, with your feet well braced and simply force the board to turn with everything your thighs and feet can give, using the boom as your lever. It takes a lot of practice!

Tacking is hard when the wind is strong.

Bearing away puts great strain on your arms. >

Gybing

This really takes some skill. Not initially, for you simply let go of the rig with your sheet hand and the sail will fly around the front of the mast. But

trying to get it back on again when the gybe is complete is something else. You need to get up out of your crouched position a little in order to grab the boom as it comes over the other side, but the moment you grab it, the sail will fill with wind and the pressure will be on. The secret is a fast gybe, with the sail pulled down over your head again as quickly as possible, and your body weight right back on the board. It sounds a contradiction in terms, but with practice it will become second nature.

A flare or jump gybe is often the best for fast manoeuvering in strong winds. The technique for this type of gybe is described in Chapter 6.

Hydroplaning

When running before the wind at high speeds, the board will tend to rock from side to side or heel dangerously one way. When this happens, the daggerboard acts like a hydroplane fin, pushing the board up onto its rails and into a total capsize, or causing it to sway dramatically from side to side with equally disastrous results.

The real answer to this problem lies with special daggerboards which do not hydroplane, but since this is not a very practical solution for the average sailboarding enthusiast, the best compromise lies in raising the daggerboard or taking it right out of its slot. This will reduce the hyroplaning tendency quite considerably and is the normal practice for running free when the daggerboard should be raised as its effectiveness is considerably reduced.

Gusts and lulls

Strong winds are never even and consistent. They tend to change speed and direction all the time. Indeed, most strong winds come in a series of gusts and lulls, particularly in sheltered water where hills or trees interfere with the even flow of the wind. Each gust invariably causes a slight change in wind direction, so if you are racing you need to be aware of such changes. The lull that follows the gust may well change the wind back to its original direction.

Much of the skill of sailing in strong winds is being able to cope with the gusty conditions. Watch the water to windward, for an approaching gust will reveal itself by a patch of small ripples that darken the surface (hence the term 'darkies'). Once you get to pick these patches,

you can watch them approach and brace the sail down ready to counter the stronger winds they bring. Experienced sailboarders use these darkies to great advantage when racing, for the board can be sailed momentarily higher into the wind when a gust strikes, thus gaining a windward advantage.

A flare gybe is spectacular in a good breeze.

6. Having Fun—Freestyle Techniques

Every sport has its fun side. With snow-skiing it's hot dogging. With water-skiing it's barefoot. With surfing it's everything you can think of.

Sailboarding is no exception and the fun side of this sport covers a multitude of challenging techniques. Collectively they are known as 'freestyle', individually they can be anything from sailing backwards to standing on your head (not literally!). Take a run down to a quiet estuary any day when the wind is moderate and watch the 'cool guys' turn their boards virtually inside out. This is freestyle, and as its name denotes, there is just no limit to what you can do once you start to play games with your board.

There are, however, a number of accepted freestyle techniques, so to get you on your way and give you some themes on which to play a wide number of variations, the following are the better known and more popular freestyle activities. Remember that it is not going to be easy for freestyle, like any development of a skill, demands that you have complete mastery of the basic techniques. The clown in a circus who tumbles on and off a horse is probably one of the most accomplished riders in the troupe. In the same way, you will need to have total control over your board and rig as well as complete mastery of the standard sailing skills before you attempt anything fancy.

Apart from developing your skills and having fun, freestyling can also be competitive. Indeed, it is a major part of sailboarding competitions with judging based on innovativeness as well as performing skills. Some of the finest boardsailors in the world concentrate on freestyle techniques, both to improve their basic skills and to win freestyle championships.

Head dip.

Head dip

This is one of the easier freestyle techniques, but is quite spectacular when done under fairly strong wind conditions. In fact, it is probably easier to do when the breeze is up, for it requires the sail to be pulled over your head to windward, which is normal practice in wind strengths over about 10-12 knots. As with all freestyle tricks, one of the most important requirements is a steady wind. The wind strength is less important than its consistency, for many a freestyler has come unstuck when just getting into the peak of his performance because the wind has suddenly dropped.

So pick still water and a steady breeze for this trick. The idea is for the board to sail steadily along while you arch your back and slowly lower your head backwards into the water. The procedure is as follows.

1. Get the board sailing on a reach and moving easily.
2. Lean backwards and outwards, arching your back and leaning to the full extent of your arms.
3. Slide you feet towards the lee side of the board, bending your knees and arching your back even more. You may not reach the water with your head the first time, but keep trying until you make it.
4. If you are not reaching the water, bend the sail back over your head. The mast will tilt back so be careful not to stall the board up into the wind. If you cannot reach the water with the top of your head at this stage, you had better give up until your arms grow longer!

Not true, of course. Never give up. The old adage that practise makes perfect is never more applicable than with freestyle techniques.

Sailing clew first

This is, in effect, backwards sailing, for although the board is going ahead bow first, the sail is back to front; the clew, or back corner of the sail, pointing towards the front of the board. It is an exercise in sail handling, as are many of these freestyle techniques, and as such is a good technique for improving your skills. Once again a moderate breeze that is holding steady is essential if you are new to this trick.

1. Get the board up and sailing steadily on a reach.
2. Transfer the front hand from the boom to a point low down on the mast.
3. Release the back hand and let the boom swing away, holding the mast upright with the front hand.
4. As the boom is swinging, change hands. When the boom is pointing over the bow, grab it with your free hand.
5. Stand up and pick up your normal sailing stance with both hands on the boom. The board will begin to move with the sail in the 180 degree reversed position—i.e. clew first.

Duck tack

Any form of tacking, if it is done fast and expertly, looks good. But there are some tacking techniques which can be extremely spectacular when performed well, and some of these come under the heading of freestyle even though they may be a part of your everyday sailing routine.

The duck tack has nothing to do with ducks, it is merely the term given to what conventional sailors do each time they go about—they duck under the boom as it goes from side to side. Normally sailboarders walk around the front of the boom when they tack, so the duck tack is quite a significant departure from the norm. For the uninitiated it requires confidence in your sailing ability and a good sense of balance and feel for the board. The procedure is as follows.

1. Sail the board into the close hauled position as normal before attempting any sort of a tack.
2. Tilt the mast back and head up into the wind as for a normal tack, but do not move towards the mast, rather move back a little towards the stern.

Duck tack.

< *Sailing clew first.*

1. Set the board up on a close reach or close haul ready to go into the tacking routine in the normal fashion.
2. Tilt the mast back, sheet on and send the board up into the wind as with a normal tack.
3. When the board is up into the wind, let go with the back hand and spin around with your back to the mast until you can grab the mast with your back hand.
4. Let go with the front hand and continue spinning around with your back to the mast.
5. Grab the boom on the opposite side with what was the front hand (now the back hand) and tilt the mast forward.
6. Take up the normal sailing position and start sailing on the other tack.

Spin tack.

3. When the sail is luffing hard, let go your forward hand and cross it over your back hand, placing it well back along the boom. Then tilt the mast forward.
4. While the board is still head to wind, duck under the sail, grab the boom on the opposite side (you may have to momentarily let go of the rig altogether) then pull the mast and sail back.
5. Once in position, get into the normal sailing stance, sheet on and sail off on the other tack.

Spin tack

This is another spectacular form of tacking, but the action comes more from the rider than the rig, for the rig performs a fairly normal tacking action while the rider does the spin part. What it amounts to, basically, is that in the course of tacking, instead of walking around the mast, facing it in the normal fashion, you perform a spin, turning your body through 360 degrees with your back to the mast. A sort of nautical spinning the light fantastic!

This one definitely needs light winds for your first attempts.

< *Duck spin tack.*

the wind, and twisting away from the sail so that your back is towards the rig.

4. Let go with the back hand and continue your spin under the rig, reaching up with the (previous) front hand to grab the boom as soon as you are under the sail.

5. Continue your spin until right round and facing the sail on the other side. Take up the normal sailing position with both hands on the boom and get the board moving again.

Helicopter

Also known as '360', this technique involves virtually throwing the sail through 360 degrees (hence the name). The clew of the sail is run off to leeward, over the bow of the board and through the wind and back to its original position. It is a spectacular trick because once the wind gets round the sail, it really whips it across and while this is impressive in normal conditions, with a strong wind it makes a spectacular display.

It is no trick for novices, however, and even experts need to learn this one in light winds. Total control and balance are essential for at times you are performing most unnatural man-

Duckspin tack

As its name denotes, this is a combination of the duck and spin tacks. It is very spectacular as it involves ducking under the sail and at the same time performing a 360 degree spin. The procedure is more akin to the duck tack than the spin tack, since it does not involve twisting around the mast, but it does require complete balance and concentration as the rig is virtually unhanded for quite some time while you spin under the sail.

The routine is to have the board swing up into the tack, then while handing the boom up so that you can duck under the sail, you spin through a 360 degree turn and grab the rig again before it fills and gets away from you. Quite a handful! The procedure is as follows.

1. Get the board moving well in preparation for the tack.
2. Tilt the mast back, and round the board up into the wind.
3. As the sail flaps, slide your back hand back along the boom, tilting the mast directly into

Helicopter. >

oeuvres and unless you have the confidence and ability to force the rig, it will flatly reject your efforts. A lot of frustration, and a lot of duckings go into learning this technique.

1. Get the board sailing smoothly on a reach in winds of no more than 5 knots initially.

2. Ease the sheet hand out until the sail luffs, then tilt the mast well over to windward. It may be neccessary to tilt the mast well down so that it is virtually pointing into the wind.

3. Push against the sail with your back hand, at the same time rotating the sail over the boom by forcing the clew up into the wind. You may find it necessary to move forward a little for this.

4. When the clew of the sail goes through the wind, the sail will whip round and you will need to be very nimble to get round with it, retaining a hold on the boom, yet not allowing it to pull you over head first. A good technique is to extend your arms and squat to absorb the considerable momentum of the sail whipping around. This is the most difficult part of the whole routine and takes a lot of practice.

5. Stand up and take up the normal sailing position.

Back-to-back

This is a very 'show-off' routine, but neverthless demands a modicum of skill. The rider stands behind the sail, on the lee side, with his back braced against the rig, arms folded and as casual as you like. Rather along the lines of the 'look Mum, no hands' attitude on a bicycle!

But for all its relaxed appearance, back-to-back sailing requires a considerable amount of skill and a great deal of confidence in your sailing ability. Although you are using no hands and no arms, you must be able to sense wind changes and the need for sail adjustments just as much as in conventional sailing, and what is more, you must apply those adjustments by simply using your back!

Getting into the back-to-back position is the first problem. The best method is as follows.

1. Get the board sailing steadily on a reach.

2. Ease off your back hand to allow the sail to luff, and with that same hand reach over and grasp the mast firmly.

3. Pass your back leg around the mast and shuffle around until you are standing on the lee side of the sail with your back to it. It will be necessary to change hands behind your back at some stage as you slide around to the lee side.

4. Brace your feet firmly on the board, slide your back hand along the boom and start to sheet in by pushing backwards with the back hand. At the same time tilt the mast forward.

5. When the board is moving, sail it as normal, using your back and mast hand for steering adjustments and your back and back hand for sheeting. Apart from feeling all back to front, one of the problems with this system is that the pressures are all the wrong way, and unless you are well braced, you will inevitably take a head-first ducking as the sail and heel of the board pitch you overboard!

Flare

This is a strong-wind technique and really requires a strong-wind daggerboard if it is to be done successfully. While you can practise in light to moderate winds, the spectacular effect is not achieved unless the board is moving fast.

1. Ease the board away into a broad reach and pick up speed.
2. As the board gets moving fast, squat down a little, then spring backwards landing squarely on the stern. At the same time pull the boom up hard. The board will skid along with the bow pointing high in the air.
3. The main requirements for success with this trick are high speed and a good breeze to keep you moving. The jump to the back of the board needs to be precise, for if the board is tilted either way, it will screw around.

Flare.

Step or Flare gybe

A development of the flare technique, this gybe is widely used and is very spectacular when done properly in strong winds. It is a technique used by wave-jumpers and other boards when tacking is difficult, or where quick manoeuvring is required, for it whips the board around smartly and looks very impressive. As its name denotes, the routine begins as a flare but is developed into a gybe by placing the weight on the back of the board to the windward side, thus utilising the harsh turn which was avoided in the flare itself.

1. Ease away to a broad reach and get up good speed.
2. Step or jump back as described for a normal flare manoeuvre.
3. When stepping to the back of the board, place the weight on the windward foot and screw the board into a gybe, at the same time tilting the mast to windward.
4. Release the back hand and carry out a fast gybe as the board flips around at high speed.
5. When the sail flips around, move forward quickly, grab the boom and push hard with your (new) windward foot to stop the turn.

Flare gybe.

Pirouette.

6. Settle the board down on the new tack and continue sailing.

Most of the problems with this type of gybe are the result of the speed with which it is executed, and you need to move forward fast after the gybe to prevent the board from turning 180 degrees when it spins round.

Body spin or Pirouette

Unlike the various spectacular tacks and gybes in freestyle techniques, the body spin, or 'pirouette' has little use in normal sailing. It is just a skilful and quite graceful trick of use only in freestyle competition or for personal satisfaction. It involves the rider performing a body spin or pirouette on the board, rotating on the ball of his back foot while the board continues to sail ahead.

Railriding.

Apart from requiring extremely good balance and a certain amount of empathy with ballet, this routine also calls for very tough feet, for unless you wear shoes, a few turns on the non-skid surface of the board will take a layer of skin off the soles of your feet!

Needless to say, this is a trick to be practised in quiet winds first of all. Similarly, the number of turns is a matter of much practice, for although skilled freestylers can continue through more than one spin, a single pirouette is usually as much as the average boardrider can handle.

1. Get the board sailing smoothly in moderate winds and on calm waters, preferably on a reach.
2. Ease back on the sheet hand to allow the sail to luff a little, and tilt the mast to windward so

that it remains upright briefly when you let it go. You may need to practise this part for some time before moving on.

3. When you feel the rig is settled, let go and spin around clockwise on the ball and toes of your back foot. Initially you will need your arms to help you turn, but for the correct performance of this routine, the arms should be crossed on the chest.
4. As the spin is completed, swing out your front leg to slow the turn, and grab the boom with both hands.
5. Resume the normal sailing position.

Railriding

The most spectacular and popular of all freestyle routines, railriding, as its name denotes, involves sailing the board on its edge or rail. It is a difficult technique and should be practised first in quiet winds and water. Since it is totally unlike any other freestyle trick, you will need to learn a whole new routine rather than adapting one of the other tricks.

1. Get the board moving steadily on a reach.
2. Place your back foot down to leeward, holding yourself steady with the rig.
3. Hook the toes of your front foot under the windward side of the board, squat down and flip the board up onto its leeward rail, jumping up onto the windward (now upper) rail with your front leg. You will need to use the rig to take a lot of the weight as you complete this manoeuvre. But as the board comes onto its rail, some of the weight can be taken on your front leg.
4. Lift your back foot up onto the top rail of the board, and using the boom, pull yourself back upright. Take up the normal sailing position, albeit with legs slightly bent and with the mast resting against the top of the tilted board.
5. As the board begins to move, you may find it easier to control the balance by occasionally placing your front foot on the daggerboard. It is also a lot more comfortable than the rail after a period of time, but be careful not to break it off or damage the slot.

7. Sailboarding Safety

Like any water sport, sailboarding can, under certain circumstances, be dangerous. Under normal conditions it is probably one of the safest of all sailing or boating activities and has many advantages over conventional sailing in yachts, catamarans or centreboarders.

For example, the sailboard cannot sink or even swamp, so no matter what emergency arises, the board will always be there as a floating survival platform. Nor can it be dismasted or grounded or set on fire. Nor, for that matter can it suffer any of the other problems which affect larger craft. Indeed the only real disadvantage with a sailboard is that it is less manoeuvrable and more prone to spills when handled by any but experienced riders.

This is where the crux of the safety side of sailboarding lies. It requires more experience and more skill to handle a board safely than does a more forgiving craft such as a sailing dinghy or keel yacht. Conventional craft, being equipped with rudders, can manoeuvre more quickly than a sailboard, and a novice sailor in an emergency situation has only to remember the basic drill of 'put the tiller in the direction of the danger' and the boat immediately turns out of the danger.

But the novice sailboarder in the same situation will not always get out of danger so easily, for lacking a tiller, he must manoeuvre the entire rig

---

The off-shore sailor must be particularly safety conscious.

in order to get out of trouble. Chances are, particularly in a fresh breeze, he will either have difficulty getting the board to respond quickly, or, if he is inexperienced, he will fall off. The latter may, of course, be one way out of the problem, but not if he is under the bow of a massive container ship!

There are other dangers, too. Most yachts and sailboats have at least some form of shelter on board, so that if a mishap occurs, the occupants can huddle out of the wind and weather until rescuers arrive. Not so with a sailboard. The sailboard rider who is unable to get his craft back to shore, must lie on top of the board, fully exposed to the elements, until help arrives.

Because of these factors, it is important that when you first begin to sail your board you learn the basic principles of sailboard safety. There is always a possibility that while you are sailing an emergency may arise, but if you are prepared for it, both physically and mentally, then you will be better able to cope with it and the chances of real danger will be considerably reduced.

Falling off is an unglamorous but effective way of stopping!

Experience

As mentioned earlier, the first important safety factor is experience. Without total control of your sailboard you are a menace to yourself and to others. This may sound a little trite, but it is very true and very important. A runaway sailboard in fresh winds could kill a swimmer very easily. Similarly a board out of control in the path of a hydrofoil or container ship could kill its rider with equal ease. Until you gain this all-important experience a basic rule of safety is to stay in a sheltered bay and stay away from other people and craft.

Many beaches and swimming areas do not permit sailboarding within a hundred metres or so of the shore, and rightly so. Everyone who has watched learners getting the hang of their board has seen the enormous whack with which a dropped mast hits the water. That same mast on a child's head could cause serious injury. There is probably no experienced sailboarder who has not seen an accident of this type, where a falling rig or runaway board has caused injury. During my early training a swimmer struck by a trainee's mast had to be taken to hospital with severe head

An experienced sailboarder has his craft always under control.

injuries. It was not really the fault of the sailboarder, except, of course, that he should not have been practising in an area frequented by swimmers.

Emergency stopping

Because of the erratic behaviour of sailboards in the hands of inexperienced riders, it is essential that you train and practise well away from other water users. And one of the early routines that should be part of your training programme is stopping the board quickly and positively. This is where sailboards have a distinct advantage over other sailcraft, for the easiest and most effective way to stop is to simply drop the rig in the water.

I always remember when learning to snow-ski, I was terrified of not being able to stop when on a fast downhill run. To this day, when I find myself getting out of control on a fast traverse, I can hear the voice of my Austrian instructor yelling 'Aboort! Aboort!' This, he explained, simply meant—'sit down!' It was a most unglamorous, but very practical way of stopping a runaway skier.

So too with dropping the rig of your sailboard. It will not win points for polished technique, but until you learn the more advanced methods, it is an extremely effective way of stopping the board.

Emergency stop.

And after all, where there is potential danger and possible injury, any system that is effective, no matter how unglamorous, is the one to use.

The technique used by most experienced sailboarders to stop the board quickly is to reverse the sail pressure by pushing the sail against the wind. This is, in effect, an adaptation of the method known as 'heaving to' which is used to stop conventional sailcraft and where the sail is 'backed' against the wind. Getting the wind on the wrong side of the sail reverses the power direction and brings the board to an immediate halt.

The procedure is as follows.

1. If the board is reaching or running, simply step forward with the back foot, push the boom hard away with the back hand until the wind is on the wrong side of the sail.
2. When the sail is firmly backed against the wind, push hard with both hands on the boom.

With practice you will be able to control the board very effectively with this method of stopping. Bear in mind, however, that the pressure in the sail will be suddenly reversed and will probably upset your balance. Until you get the hang of the fast stopping technique you will probably experience a few duckings!

Check your gear

Once you have mastered the handling and control of the board you can set off on extended runs across open water. But before setting off each time, it is an important safety routine to check that your gear is in order. Now that you have confidence in yourself, you must also have confidence in your board, for nothing is more demoralising—and frightening—when you are still a novice, than to be half way across a stretch of open water, well away from assistance, and have a vital part of the gear break or carry away.

A quick check of the gear before you set off takes but a few minutes and can avoid a great deal of trauma. Even new equipment can give trouble, and gear which is well used must always be closely checked to ensure that it has not worn to the point of breaking. A basic routine for checking the sailboard and gear before an extended sail would be as follows.

- Check out the board for cracks or dents which have broken the skin. Particularly examine the area around the daggerboard slot and the mast step as these are stress areas.
- Examine the skeg for looseness or damage and ensure that the plug is firmly in place.
- Check out the action of the universal joint and examine it for wear.
- Check the fitting of the mast step. This is an area that wears quickly. If it is loose in its socket, tape it or wrap a piece of rag around it.
- A loose mast step makes raising the mast very difficult.
- Check the mast and boom for signs of wear, cracking or other damage.
- Examine all lines for chafe or damage. Worn inhauls and outhauls tend to slip out of their cleats very easily.
- Worn cleat grips can create the same problem, so check those as well.
- Check the sails for damage or loose stitching, particularly in the region of the batten pockets.
- Check the battens to ensure they are not cracked or warped (full width battens).
- Rig the board and give it an overall check, looking particularly for any looseness or sloppiness which may indicate wear.

Clothing

The right type of clothing is much more important for sailboarding than it is for conventional sailing. Frequent immersion and constant exposure to the elements is a feature of sailboarding and this can take a severe toll of your skin and body unless adequate protection is provided in the form of correct clothing.

There are two major hazards related to the sort of exposure you will experience when sailboarding—skin damage due to sun, and body damage due to cold. Both can create discomfort, both can cause severe illness, even death. It goes without saying, then, that both must be very much in mind when sailboarding.

Excessive exposure to the sun will lead at least

Checking the gear

to skin damage, at worst to melanoma, a potentially terminal skin cancer. Since protection from the sun is relatively easy, you would be foolish indeed to risk health problems by not taking steps to avoid such risks. Even in temperate climates precautions must be taken, for on the water the sun's rays are exacerbated by reflections from the water, the board and the sails. Overcast and cool days are deceptive and the damaging ultra-violet rays may be just as strong on those days as they are on the more obvious days when the sun is bright and burning.

Depending on conditions, one or all of the following should be used to reduce the inensity of the sun the skin when sailboarding.

- T-shirt or some other form of body covering for the upper abdomen should be worn at all times in summer, and throughout the year in warmer

1. The gear must be correctly rigged from step one.

2. Adjustment of the sail for weather conditions is a last minute procedure.

3. Lines must be properly secured.

4. Lifting the rig will indicate how the sail sets.

Wetsuit 'skins' are ideal for most sailboarding conditions.

In conditions like these, body and skin protection is essential.

climates. Long-leg shorts (board shorts) or some other covering for the thighs is important as these are particularly prone to melanomas.

- Hat or visor or some other means of protecting the face which catches all the reflections from the sail, board and water. Because a hat is easily lost when you fall in the water, or may be blown off when you get up speed, it will need to be tied on with elastic or tape.

- Sunglasses are optional, because they are very difficult to keep on, particularly when sailing hard. However, constant severe glare can damage your eyes, so some form of protection is necessary. New types of sunglasses designed for water sports stay on even when you take a ducking.

- Blocking creams, while not exactly clothing, are an essential form of protection when sailboarding. Use the highest category (i.e. the

one with the greatest protection) and one which is reasonably waterproof. Use it liberally and frequently on your face and other exposed areas.

Excessive cold can be as dangerous as excessive sunlight, particularly in cooler regions where constant immersion and exposure to cooling winds creates a refrigerator-like situation in which the interior of the body very quickly loses heat as it is evaporated out through the skin. A condition known as hypothermia can develop in which the body heat evaporates to the extent that the internal organs may cease to function. This is obviously a very severe condition and may lead to death.

Although this problem occurs more in temperate and cool climates, even warm and tropical climates are not without risk. A sailboarder who for some reason cannot get back to shore can, if he is not correctly clothed, suffer hypothermia as a result of constant immersion and cooling as he lies on his board exposed to all the elements, even though the temperature of the air is quite high. So it is a factor to be considered wherever you sail, but is obviously of prime importance in cool climates.

Once again the answer lies with clothing. For close inshore sailing where you are unlikely to be out of reach of the shore for very long, a T-shirt may be sufficient protection for the cool breeze as well as for sunlight. Where you expect to be sailing for some time, or where you are in an offshore situation where, in an emergency, help could be a long time in arriving, you need to be protected by a wetsuit.

Wetsuits range in thickness and fashion to suit different sailing conditions and climates. Apart from choosing the thickness and design most suited to your type of sailing, it is important to ensure that the suit fits tightly on all parts of your body. A loose wetsuit is of no use, since the principle of the wetsuit involves locking an insulating layer of water around your body to prevent the escape of body heat. If that layer of water is allowed to circulate, as it will inside a loose suit, it will have the opposite effect, and carry away your body heat rather than retain it.

Lifejackets

Lifejackets, or some other form of buoyancy, are often required by law. Even if not mandatory in the area where you are sailing, you should give careful consideration to the practice of wearing some sort of buoyancy gear. Although it perhaps seems a bit extreme to wear a lifejacket when you are sailing only a few hundred metres from the shore, you are a good swimmer, and the board itself is an excellent survival platform, it is important to do so. There is always the possibility that as a result of an accident you could be uncon-

---

A good wetsuit must fit tightly without being restrictive or pinching.

Lifejackets are often compulsory.

scious when you fall in the water and the support of a buoyancy vest could save your life.

However, full buoyancy lifejackets which support an unconscious victim with his or her head above water are bulky and cumbersome and make it very difficult to get back on the board after falling in the water. The type of buoyancy vest normally worn on sailboards is much less bulky but does not have full support for an unconscious victim. So it is a bit of a Hobson's choice. The sensible approach is to wear a sailboarding lifejacket at all times when required by law or when sailing some distance from shore. When the law does not require it and you are a good swimmer, then it is not so essential. The sailboard itself, as mentioned, is an excellent survival platform and problems with sailboarders close to shore are rare.

Watch the weather

Since the weather is the factor most influencing any kind of water sport, it makes good sense to check the forecast before you go sailboarding. Like catamarans and centreboards, sailboards are very susceptible to fresh winds, and most novice sailors have trouble coping with more than around 10 knots of wind. As important as the wind strength is its direction, for an offshore breeze can create problems, even dangers, for inexperienced board riders, whereas there are less problems associated with onshore breezes.

Telephone, television and newspaper forecasts are usually taken directly from the Bureau of Meteorology and therefore are reasonably reliable for some hours ahead. If you are relatively inexperienced, avoid sailing in fresh offshore winds or conditions that may result in an offshore wind strengthening. More sailboarders get into trouble through being blown offshore than for any other single reason, and when the wind freshens to the point where you can no longer sail home against it, the chances are it will also be too strong for you to paddle back.

Watch out also for fronts, particularly cold fronts, which can bring violent thunderstorms with them, to say nothing of hail, rain and even lightning. As a rule the forecast will issue in advance warnings of strong winds or violent

frontal conditions, but local 'nasties' can spring up unexpectedly at any time and in any conditions. A wise procedure is to keep an eye attuned to the sky in the west (most weather conditions move from west to east) or whichever direction the prevailing bad weather comes from. The approach of bad weather is usually well indicated by cloud formations and if you get to know your clouds, you will soon learn to interpret the sky signs and predict approaching weather with some degree of accuracy.

Emergency

Emergencies on sailboards are rare, the most common, as described earlier, relating to inexperienced boardriders being blown out to sea by strong offshore winds. However, gear failure or some other unexpected problem can also make it difficult, perhaps impossible to get back to shore, so it is important to know what to do when an emergency occurs.

There are numerous emergency signals for craft on the water, but none really apply to sailboards since you cannot carry flares or other signalling apparatus on board as can larger craft. If you are in trouble on your sailboard, the only effective method of signalling for help is to stand upright on the board and wave with both arms over your head. Anyone in sight, weather nautically orientated or not, will recognise this as a signal of distress.

If the wind dies and you cannot get back to the beach, or if you have some kind of gear failure, it is relatively easy to paddle the board. You must first unrig by releasing the uphaul and outhaul, removing the boom and battens, and rolling the sail tightly around the mast. Then pull mast and boom onto the board, lie down on your stomach and start to paddle with both arms. If you have a removable daggerboard, use it as a paddle, but it is suprising how fast a board will move just by paddling with your hands and arms. Of course it is a tiring process, particularly if you have a head wind. Often it is best to look for a shore which is across wind, even if it is further away, and head for that. Paddling into a stiff chop can be exhausting even for a very fit sailboarder.

If you get cold while attempting to get back to the beach or while waiting for rescue, unfurl the sail from the mast and wrap yourself in it. The Dacron of the sailcloth provides a good windbreak and will help your wetsuit keep out the cold. Remember that it is of vital importance to keep warm when any emergency arises, for hypothermia can strike quickly when you are cold and exhausted.

Panic

This is the worst aspect of all when an emergency arises. Panic kills more people than any other factor and it is essential to your survival that you remain rational and calm or you may make the situation far worse than it is. Above all, resist the urge to leave the board and swim for a nearby shore. No matter how close that shore appears, it will always be further than you think, and even if exhaustion does not get you, there are unseen dangers such as currents or sharks which may make their presence felt before you reach the shore.

A sailboard is a good survival platform, and the moment you let go of it you have relinquished your best chance of survival. Until rescue is right there with you, or your feet can touch bottom, remember the old maxim:

STAY WITH THE BOARD

Sooner or later you will be missed and searchers will come looking for you. A floating sailboard is far easier to spot than a head in the water. It would be grim irony if your rescuers found your board, but failed to find you because you had swum away from it. Sharks cannot eat sailboards but they can eat humans. As long as you are atop the board no marine predator can get at you, nor can the sea drown you. Your board is your insurance policy. Stick with it!

Most dangers occur in offshore waters.

8. Preparing to Race

Although not everyone likes racing, few people can resist a challenge. Sailboarders are no exception and inevitably, as you get to master the various techniques of the sport, you will begin to pit your skills against others. Initially it will probably just be a few fun races with mates of similar standards, but eventually your newly found prowess will need the stimulus of greater challenge and you will start to enter the competitive side of the sport.

There are a number of ways you can get into racing, but the best is through a club or association. Some of the widely established boards such as Windsurfer and Dufor have associations which organise class racing. Starting with just local races among association members, one-design class racing can be developed through inter-club, State and national racing to international one-design class racing and ultimately to the Olympic Games.

However, not all sailboard competition revolves around one-design class racing. There is open class racing and development class racing to mention but two others. Sailboard regattas are held, usually during summer, by many clubs and associations in which one-design as well as other types of racing is involved. While one-design classes are usually more predominant, particularly in national and international competition, nevertheless there is excellent competitive sport in other types of racing.

One-design class racing, where each board and its rig is strictly measured and controlled so that all are precisely the same, is without question the most popular. With the boards and rigs exactly the same, the outcome of the race depends solely on the sailboarder, which makes for highly competitive challenge racing.

Most sailboard races are controlled by the International Yacht Racing Union (IYRU), as indeed are most yacht races. This ensures that competitions run in any part of the world are controlled by the one body and no nation or competitor gains an unfair advantage. The rules for international sailboard racing are laid down by the IYRU and these are usually followed by all racing bodies, from international right down to basic club or association level. It goes without saying that the rules must be read and understood by every sailboarder intending to start racing.

Getting started

There are two ways in which to get started when you feel you have reached the degree of proficiency required for competitive racing. The first is to join a club or association which runs sailboard races. The second is to get yourself orientated to racing, which is far removed from the casual 'social' sailing you have enjoyed since learning to sail. Joining a club or association should not be difficult, but getting orientated to racing is a long, hard haul.

Firstly, as mentioned earlier, you must read and inwardly digest the rule book until you are completely familiar with the clauses which will apply to your type of racing. Tactics, which is in effect the use of the rules to gain an advantage over a competitor, are a major part of racing, and you will only develop good tactical ability when you know every rule in the book and know it backwards. Although sailing ability is obviously a prime factor in any race, a clever tactician can often outwit even the best sailor.

Once you are familiar with the theory, then get started on the practice. The best way to learn how to race is to enter as a competitor, but hang back from the start, then follow the race around the course and watch how the experts do it. If you plunge right in to racing before you are orientated, you will not only get totally confused, but you will also upset the front runners by your

confusion, which will not make you popular in the clubhouse. By sitting back and watching the start, then following the race around the course, watching and analysing the moves of the leaders on each leg and at each mark, you will soon begin to understand the various moves and counter-moves.

Then go home and read a few good books on racing to see how these factors affect a racing sailboarder and give him or her an edge on competitors. Between reading at home, and watching in practice on the race course, you will soon start to develop your own ideas and tactics. As you do so, you can start to enter more fully into the race. Instead of hanging back, move up with the starters when the gun goes off. Get in amongst the experts and challenge them (correctly, of course) and see what tactics they take to meet your challenge.

While on the subject of experts, there is no better source of information on racing than the experts themselves. Corner them in the bar. Buy them a drink. Flatter them on their prowess. Play to their egos (all good performers are egoists!) and you will find hints and tips falling from their lips like raindrops. Gather them up and take them home. One day you may use them to beat the pants off the expert whose brains you picked!

The Olympic course

Most conventional races are run around a course roughly in the form of an isosceles triangle, one leg of which is directly into the wind. This is known as an Olympic course from its use in the Olympic Games, and is so designed that it tests the competitors on every point of sailing.

As a rule, the start is to windward and the

starting line is therefore directly across wind. This means that the sailboards must tack over the start line, and provides the most exciting and spectacular start to a race, with sailboards jockeying and jostling for favoured positions and favoured tacks. The first leg of the course will be a windward leg which means that all boards must tack or beat to windward—the most testing of all forms of sailing.

At the end of the windward leg the boards close in around the windward mark, usually a buoy of some form, and jostle for favoured positions to begin the second leg, usually a reach. At the end of the reaching leg another mark forms the turning point for the third leg which is either a reach on the opposite tack, or sometimes a run. Either way, the turn at the leeward mark involves a gybe.

The third leg comes back to the starting buoy, from where, as a general rule, a further one or two windward legs are run. This ensures that the race both starts and finishes with the most testing form of sailing. The finish is usually at the end of

The best way to learn is to watch!

the windward leg, although in some local racing the start line may double as the finish line, depending on the waterway in use and, to a certain extent, on the weather.

Preparing the board

If you are to get the best out of your sailboard when racing, then it must be in the best possible condition. That does not mean that it must be in new condition. Far from it. A sailboard which has been well tried and tested and honed to a high racing pitch will often turn in a better performance than one which has just come off the shelf. But it does mean that the sails and the board, as well as all the ancillary gear, must be set and tuned to perfection with even the slightest flaws removed.

The sails, for example, must be in excellent condition, not stretched or baggy from over-use. They must be set so that all wrinkles are removed, particularly those at the corners and along the luff or leading edge. This means using good lines for the outhaul, downhaul and inhaul, preferably pre-stretched, braided rope which will not allow

the sail to change shape once it has been firmly set.

The shape of the sail is important to the speed of the board, and this shape can be changed by varying the tension on the lines. In strong weather the downhaul and outhaul should be pulled as tight as possible to ensure that the sail is as flat as possible. In lighter winds, these lines are slacked a little to allow the shape of the sail to fall into more of a curve. In this shape it gathers up more air and transmits more power to the board. In high winds it may be necessary to change down to a smaller sail, even a storm sail to prevent the board being overpowered and hard to manage.

The board itself should be as flat as possible to obtain the greatest speed. This is definitely not a time to 'scoop' the bow or bend the stern, for the longer the length of board in the water, the faster it goes. Scratches, grooves and dents on the underside of the sailboard will create surface friction with the water which results in drag and

The beach on race day is busy.

slower speed. Such damage must be sanded down and repaired and then the bottom of the board polished to obtain the smoothest possible surface. If there are no scratches it is still a wise procedure to polish the bottom surface to reduce drag to an absolute minimum.

The daggerboard and skeg must be firmly fitted, the former by means of tape if it tends to move when in the lowered position. The shape of the daggerboard will be determined by the type of racing and the strength of the wind, so if you have an interchangeable daggerboard, you will need to select the appropriate one when getting the sailboard ready for racing. The class rules will indicate what can and what cannot be used.

The gear checks mentioned in Chapter 7 will cover most other pre-race requirements. But make sure that little things such as the grip on the booms and the non-skid surface on the board are

Final checks before take-off are vital.

adequate. Nothing is worse than to be well placed in a race, then lose the whole thing because you cannot keep your grip, either with hands or feet, and keep falling off. Similarly, ensure that the universal joint, cleats and bungees are all in good condition, for you will curse yourself if you lose the race through some minor oversight.

Preparing yourself

Getting yourself ready for a race does not mean just putting on the right clothes. It means 'psyching' yourself to a pitch where you are mentally ready to do battle with other sailboarders, all just as intent as you on winning the race. They will all be psyched up and tensed ready for the fray, every nerve honed to react quickly and smoothly to any situation which might gain them an advantage. If you just breeze into the line-up with a casual, indifferent attitude, you will be left behind on the starting line when the gun goes off.

Just as the powerful motor of a racing car takes a little time to get warmed up and giving of its best, so it takes the human mind a little while to get into gear and build up to give its best when the race commences. Your concentration must be at a peak, for to miss a move by one of what might be dozens of competitors may mean losing one place in the race. Your mind must be sharp and alert, your concentration intense, and your reflexes in a state of immediate readiness. Only then are you ready to line up for the starting gun.

How to get into this finely tuned state of men-

tal readiness is a matter for personal application. The method I have found best is to get out on the water well before the race starts and go into a series of routines which will tune up your mind as well as your body. It is important, anyway, to take the board for a thorough test sail before the start, as we shall see later. Use that time to prepare yourself mentally, sweeping the board through a series of intricate manoeuvres until you feel total confidence that she is moving faster and better than ever before.

Often you will find other boardriders out there doing the same thing. Pit yourself against a few of them and 'burn them off'. Regardless of their degree of skill, the more you fly past, the more your confidence will grow. You may well find some of them appreciating the chance of a tune-up challenge, in which case you can engage in some pre-race 'dices'—an excellent way to get your mind and body honed to a fine edge. By the time the race starts you will be mentally straining at the leash!

Pre-race check

Like every racing machine, a sailboard needs a thorough pre-race check to ensure that everything is working smoothly before the starter's gun goes off. The static check of gear on the beach is important, but the final check on the water with the board under full pressure of wind is the only

Limbering up is a good physical and mental exercise.

Too late now to find you left something behind.

way to ensure that every aspect has been checked out and nothing overlooked.

It is an important check also to ensure that you have tuned the sail correctly for the weight of breeze, for often the breeze on the beach is totally different to that out on the bay. If you make your pre-race check early, there is still time to make adjustments or even, if necessary, run back to the beach and change the sail. Only when the sail is full of wind will aggravating items—so easily overlooked, but which could cost you the race—show up.

Take the board well out from the shore to check the wind. If you have time, it might even be a good idea to sail the first leg of the course, for then you will know exactly what to expect when the race starts. Throw the board around through all possible manoeuvres until you feel totally confident in your handling ability. With dozens of other boards around you in the race, you will need to be just that much quicker and smoother in your actions than when you are practicing alone. As you build up your confidence you will also give the gear a thorough check under race conditions, so that by the time you return to the starting line, both you and your sailboard will be confident and ready.

9. Racing

With everything tuned to perfection, the pre-race checks completed and your mind psyched up for the race, you are ready for the start. It will mostly be a windward start, which means a tack or beat to windward along the first leg, then a reach and a further reach or run to complete the triangular course. While every part of the race will have an important bearing on the outcome, probably none is more important than the start. Getting a good start not only gets you out into a clear wind away from the turbulence and frustra-

tion of sailing among the mob, but also gives you an enormous psychological boost. For this reason, it is worth spending some considerable time and effort on getting a good start.

The start line

Although not every race starts to windward, it is the most popular way to start short races, particularly those around an Olympic course. The start line is laid across the wind, and all sailboards participating in the race manoeuvre behind the line prior to the starter's gun being fired. A variety

The starter's boat will be positioned near the end of the start line.

Pre-race manoeuvering can make a great difference to the start.

of signals may be used to time the approach of the start, mostly flags indicating each minute from about 10 or 15 minutes prior to the start gun. As each minute passes, the relative flag is lowered and another hoisted in its place. A gun may be fired or hooter sounded at the 5-minute mark and again at the 1-minute mark, but these signals may vary according to the decisions of the race committee.

The starting line is usually marked by two buoys, one at each end, and although it lies across wind, the line is usually angled slightly so that one end is upwind of the other. The upwind, or 'favoured' end is obviously the one to aim for since it lies slightly closer to the first mark. Needless to say, every sailboard in the race will also head for that end of the line, hence the 'bunching' that often occurs as the gun is about to go off. Less experienced sailors should avoid starting at the favoured end or they will find themselves left wallowing in the foul air and wash of the experts. A good start in clear air, even if it is somewhat farther down the line, is preferable.

To determine the favoured end of the line, sail towards it during your pre-race manoeuvres, first on one tack and then the other. When you are on the line, hold the mast upright on the board and turn into the wind until the sail luffs. Repeat this procedure on the opposite tack. The buoy which is closest to the bow when the sail is luffing is at the favoured end of the line.

Pre-race manoeuvering

It is important to use the period prior to the start gun to get yourself and your board into a favourable starting position. If, when the gun is fired, your bow is over the line, you will be recalled and must return behind the line for another start. That, of course, is disasterous since the rest of the fleet will be away and gone by the time you cross the line for a second start.

By the same token, it is important to be as close to the line as possible when the gun is fired, or you will find yourself left in the foul or 'dirty' air of the other competitors and unable to get your board moving. This air is the result of turbulence from other sails to windward, and can result either in total blanketing, which means your board will go nowhere, or a series of whirling air currents which will give you a very hard time as they rapidly change direction and speed.

So two factors emerge as the secret to a good start—crossing the line right on the gun, and staying in clear air. Easier said than done when perhaps one hundred boards are all trying to do the same thing. But this is the secret of the start, and much of the success will be determined by your pre-race manoeuvres. During the minutes prior to the gun, determine just where you plan to cross the line. Make several runs at it so that you get to judge your board's speed. Determine at what distance behind the line you will begin your run.

Most racing boardriders prefer to lie right on the line in a static condition, then pull on their sails at the moment the gun is fired. Others get moving and judge their speed so that at the instant the gun is fired, their board is travelling across the line at full speed, leaving the others wallowing. This, of course, takes a great deal of fine judgement and practise.

If you go for the favoured end of the line, watch out for 'barging'. This is an illegal tactic but is widely practiced and often hard to avoid. It occurs when boards outside the mark try to push between the boards starting close to the mark and the mark itself. It is a good reason for avoiding the favoured end of the starting line unless you are a very experienced race sailor.

Whatever the tactics you adopt, use the pre-race manoeuvring times to get yourself in the right position for the start you intend to make. There will be a lot of milling around as others do the same, so keep a close eye out to see that no bunching commences, for if it does, you will need to be well clear of it. Timing is very important and a stop watch will help you judge the time you have for this pre-race manoeuvring.

The start

Probably the best way to start is to have your board moving fast across the line at the moment the gun goes off, for this gives you the jump on competitors lying static on the line. However, it

Bunching like this creates very disturbed air.

takes extremely good judgement to do this, to say nothing of finding a spot to break through the mob on the line. With large starting fleets the most popular method is the static start where you merely drift close to the start line, hold the board static until the gun goes off, then sheet on hard to get the jump on the others. For the uninitiated, the static start is the best. Until you become experienced, the flying start is fraught with problems, not least of which is 'breaking' the line before the gun goes off.

Having, during the pre-race manoeuvres, decided on just where you intend to make your start, work your board slowly up to that position on the line. If you have raced a lot before, you will be heading for the windward or favoured end of the line with a view to starting on a starboard or 'favoured' tack. The advantages of starting at the favoured end have already been described, and the advantage of the starboard tack is that

you have right of way over all boards starting on a port tack. In the tight formation of the start, having right of way gives you enormous advantages for in the close tacking duels that develop after the race has started, all port tack boards will have to pass behind you, thus giving you an advantage of distance and also of clear wind.

If you are fairly new to racing, however, it is better to start further down the line away from the favoured end. Here there will be more space and less foul wind from other boards. Although you will not get the best start in the fleet from this position, neither will you get the worst, for the ones who will suffer most are those bunched behind the leaders, wallowing in their foul wind and wash. Still attempt to start on a starboard tack if possible, although if you are too far down the line, this tack may carry you too far out from the courseline, in which case you have no choice but to start on a port tack. These are all factors which you should have anticipated during your pre-race manoeuvres.

Of greatest importance is clear air, for without a clean wind, you will go nowhere, and if getting

Static start.

a clean wind means starting at the far end of the line, then so be it. You will find to your surprise that as the race progresses along the windward leg, far from being last because you started at the 'wrong' end of the line, there is a large segment of the fleet still behind you. Even if you have to sail away a little from the main body of the fleet, by remaining in clear air you will have gained an advantage over many a competitor who started well, but who got locked into a 'bunch'.

The windward leg

Your sole aim on the windward leg is to get to the mark before any other competitor. You cannot sail in a direct line because this leg is a beat to windward, so you must sail as close to the wind as you can, first on one tack, then on the other. The key words are *close to the wind*, for the board which sails closest to the wind will gain an advan-

Flying start.

tage on every tack and therefore reach the windward mark first.

Sailing as close to the wind as possible means first ensuring that your sail is set correctly for this condition. The boom should be kept as close to the centreline of the board as is possible under the prevailing wind conditions. The board is sailed up to the wind to the point where the sail begins to luff or the board begins to slip sideways and lose momentum, then taken off the wind again until the sail is full and the board is moving fast. This is the optimum sailing position when tacking to windward, and providing your sails are in good shape and all other factors are equal, you should sail as high into the wind as any other competitor.

If the sail is not tensioned correctly for the weight of wind, or the cloth is stretched and baggy, the luff will appear early and you will not be 'pointing' as high into the wind as you would

A busy start.

with correctly set sails. Similarly, if the mast is not upright and perpendicular to the board, the best sailing position will not be achieved. Much depends on wind conditions, of course, for in strong winds the mast must be deliberately pulled to windward. But such conditions affect the other competitors also, so it will be the racer who gets his act together best under the conditions that exist who will get to the windward mark first.

Lay lines

The biggest problem in determining your tactics on the windward leg is to know just where to make each tack. Each time you go about you slow the board down and lose ground, so in theory one big tack is the best. But in practice you will most likely need to sail a long way out on one tack in order to bring the windward mark dead ahead on the next tack, and thus complete the leg with only one change of direction. If you are way out from the courseline and the wind changes, you could find yourself at a total disadvantage with an even harder work back—a move which will almost certainly put you out of the race.

Beating along the windward leg is the most testing part of the race.

The compromise solution used by most racing sailboarders is to tack within a 'cone' configuration, the apex of which is the mark, and the limits of which are lines drawn outwards at an angle from the mark. These are known as 'lay lines' and if you tack within those lay lines you reduce your chances of being caught out by a wind shift, and improve your chances of getting to the mark first.

With this system the early legs of the windward beat are fairly long, but become shorter as the lay lines compress towards the mark. The last few tacks before rounding the mark will be made in fairly quick time.

Lifts and knocks

The wind is never constant, but varies continually both in direction and strength. The closer to land, the more the wind gusts, so that estuaries, coastal waterways and lakes—the areas most favoured by sailboarders— are very prone to gusty conditions. However, the experienced sailboarder can use these gusts to advantage, for each time the wind gusts it changes direction. If it moves closer to the bow, luffing the sail and thus making it necessary to turn away from the wind,

it is said to be 'heading' or 'knocking' the board. If it swings out onto the side, then the board can be headed up closer towards the mark, and this is termed a 'lift'. Working the gusts requires close concentration and quick reflexes, but can make all the difference when beating to windward in close competition.

Trim tricks

To attain maximum speed the board should be kept as flat on the water as possible, but in working to windward with a fresh wind, the wind chop may cause the bow to bury, thus reducing speed. It will be necessary to move back a little and tilt the bow of the board up to prevent this, although tilting must be kept to a minimum or the board will not produce its best speed. Similarly, when running downwind on wind waves, the bow may tend to bury itself in the troughs, and you will need to move aft on the board again to prevent this.

In light winds the lee rail can be dipped a little to reduce surface friction on the wetted surface, but as a general rule, the flatter the trim of the board the better for forward speed. Tilting the sail to leeward is also a light-weather practice as it helps the sail fall into its correct shape rather than hang like baggy washing from the peak.

Rounding a mark

At all turning buoys or marks you can expect to be in close company, for however scattered the fleet has been along the leg, every sailboard converges on the mark. This calls for smart action both in terms of applying the rules and thus avoiding a collision, and also in getting the board around the mark and onto the other tack. At the weather mark, sail as close to the buoy as possible, although if there is a tight bunch forming, then sweep wide a little to retain your clear wind. The inside board at the mark will catch all the foul wind from the others, and the board outside, although it might have slightly farther to go, will have a totally clear wind and be able to rocket around. Getting into a bunch at a mark is as disastrous as getting into a bunch on the starting

Close duelling on the windward leg.

line. Better by far to stay in clear air, even if it means having further to sail.

At the leeward mark a gybe will be called for, and this will need to be executed quickly and efficiently to avoid losing ground. A good tactic here is to deliberately sweep wide on the approach, cutting hard in after the gybe in the hope of sneaking inside the bunch. A bunch often get carried a little too far as they try not to run into one another while rounding the mark.

Holding a clear wind is a big part of racing.

By staying out a little initially, there is every chance you will see a gap, and if you are in clear air and moving fast, you can nip through it.

In watching your competitors, however, do not lose sight of the mark itself. If you touch a mark in rounding, you will incur a penalty—usually re-rounding. Sailing back to a mark and re-rounding it will almost certainly put paid to your winning the race or even gaining a place.

The offwind legs

One of the major problems when reaching or running in a large group is the risk of getting 'blanketed' by boards coming up behind. If you are engaged in a one-to-one duel it is sometimes a good tactic to deliberately blanket a competitor in front of you. As he loses his wind and wallows to a halt, you will race past, a smug grin on your face. But remember he is almost certain to repay the compliment since he is now in a position to blanket you. Such cat and mouse tactics achieve nothing, for the rest of the competitors race away while you and your buddy slow each other down. The smug grins become a little strained when you discover you are the last two in the fleet!

As with any aspect of racing, staying in clear air is the secret of going fast on a downwind leg.

It is often worth easing out from the direct course-line to the mark in order to avoid the foul air of a bunch coming up behind you. Always keep a good eye on the others when reaching or running, particularly when approaching a mark, for the foul air from a bunch of sailboards can extend some distance and put you at a decided disadvantage if you fall into it.

The finish

As with the start line, the finish line is sometimes biased, and therefore will have a favoured end. Since the fleet will be more scattered at the finish than at the start, it makes good sense to head directly for the favoured end of the finish line if you see a clear run ahead. If the finish is on the downwind leg, this is one time when blanketing can be of use, but the tactic needs to be well executed. If you have a competitor up ahead,

You need to pull every trick in the book to stay with the competition.

∧ *Running down on the leeward mark.*

The windward mark is usually the first, and sorts out the field. ∨

Working close to the shoreline can often pay off.

Personal duels rarely benefit anyone but the remainder of the fleet.

maneouvre your board closer to him as the finish line approaches, then when only a few metres from the line, swing across and blanket his sail. If you have timed it correctly you will be able to race past and cross the line before he has time to pick up his wind and try the same tactic on you!

Sometimes the finish is to windward, in which case always try to make your run for the line on a starboard tack. This gives you the right of way over any other sailboard making for the line on a port tack. In hot competition this could make the difference between winning and losing.

Tactics

There is no room in a book of this nature to delve deeply into racing tactics. Suffice it to say that tactics are a vitally important part of racing and can make the difference between a mediocre performance and a good performance. Tactics mostly involve the use of the racing rules, so ensure before you start that you are totally familiar with all the rules and their application at any point in the race.

Local knowledge

Although sailboards are less affected by tides and currents than are deep-keeled sailing craft, nevertheless strong tidal conditions can make all the difference to your performance in a race. If you are racing in home waters, be sure you are familiar with the times and movement of tidal flows. If you are racing in unfamiliar waters, spend some considerable time gaining local knowledge about tides and tidal flows. A sail-board going to windward in average conditions may make a speed over the ground of only 4 knots. If it is headed by a tidal runout of 4 knots, then that board is going precisely nowhere!

Similarly with wind shifts. The topography of the surrounding countryside has much to do with the wind patterns on the water. Local sailors knowing of a 'lift' close to a certain shore, will use that to great advantage in a race. Get talking with the locals a day or two ahead of the race and know where the favoured shorelines are.

The great moment—crossing the line ahead of the fleet.

10. Wave-Sailing

To many sailboarders, wave-sailing is the ultimate sport. While normal boardsailing requires a certain amount of concentration and experience, particularly as the winds grow stronger, and freestyle demands a range of advanced skills, neither of these requires even a fraction of the concentration, skills and experience that is necessary to sail a board out and back through big surf waves. Indeed, so demanding is this aspect of sailboarding, that different skills are required for sailing out through the waves to those used when surfing back in to the beach.

And not only are different skills involved, but also different rigs are employed. While it is possible to ride very modest waves with a standard fun board, such a board is usually too long and flat and the bow sticks into the water, causing frequent spills. In addition, the standard rig is not designed for the violent stresses that occur when rocketing over a wave.

Wave boards

Unlike flat-water sailboards, which are mostly of stock design and manufacture, wave boards are usually custom made. It is possible to buy good wave-riding boards, and initially this is the best procedure. But as you become more expert you will feel the need for a board to suit your weight and style, and this usually means having it custom made.

There are two principle categories for wave boards—'floaters' and 'sinkers'. As their name denotes, they are either capable of supporting a full body weight, and can therefore be started by uphauling the sail from the water, or they are unable to support full body weight at rest and must be started with either a beach start or a water start. Some boards naturally fall between these two extremes, but most fit into one category or the other.

Wave boards are generally smaller and shorter than still-water boards. Wide boards are more

stable than narrow boards, but the latter are mostly more manoeuvrable. Similarly, boards with narrow tails manoeuvre well, but are slower to get up on the plane. The pointed 'pintail' is excellent for wave-riding as it gets a good bite on the water when turning hard and is one of the most popular design features in high performance surf-sailing. However, it lacks buoyancy and tends to sink into a wave when jumping, reducing the effect of the important 'kick-off' so necessary to get a board airborne.

Skegs are also usually different in wave boards. While some retain the conventional single skeg and daggerboard of the fun board, most wave boards opt for three skegs at the tail to provide directional stability when manoeuvering or jumping at high speed. Daggerboards are virtually useless when riding down the face of a wave, and most custom built boards discard them. The two 'wing' skegs on either side of the centre skeg ensure that even when the board is heeled hard in a tight turn, one skeg is getting a good bite on the water and preventing the tail of the board from slewing around. Often these wing skegs are turned inwards so that when they bite into the water, they also assist the turn of the board.

The trend in sails for wave sailing rigs changes frequently. A general purpose sail for moderate conditions would be about 4.9 square metres in area. Ideally, of course, you should have more than one sail to cope with the widely (and quickly) varying conditions you will encounter on a day at the beach. On an average, additional sails of 4.2 square metres and 5.6 square metres will enable you to sail in all but extreme conditions.

Some sailboarders favour the high-aspect rig with its relatively tall, narrow sail with no battens at all, especially for small waves. These are sometimes called 'pinhead' sails and although often

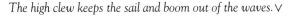

The high clew keeps the sail and boom out of the waves. ∨   *Footstraps and special skegs are a feature of wave boards.* ∧

used, suffer from the disadvantage of a long boom which makes water starts a problem. Moving much of the sail area to the top of the sail creates a narrow sail with a shorter boom but plenty of sail up high where it can catch the wind over the tops of the waves. 'Fathead' sails, as these are called, are popular for big-wave riding.

Many modern wave-riders seem to prefer smaller sails with a pronounced curve in the luff and leech and fitted with full-width battens. Apart from new developments in sail cloth and sailmaking, the different types of waves encountered in different wave-riding locations around the world have much to do with the shape of sails.

A common factor of all wave-riding rigs is the high clew which avoids the risk of dragging the boom and sail in the water. Big windows enable you to watch the approach of each wave while higher set booms allow greater purchase and keep the sail out of the water. Complete control of the sailboard is essential in wave-riding, whether the board is in or out of the water. Better control of the board is made possible by the footstraps, while sail shape is retained by the full-width battens.

First steps

Because of the different equipment and techniques used for wave-sailing, the best way to graduate from conventional still-water sailboarding is to purchase a good 'floater' wave-board and get used to it on a lake or some other still-water venue. Becoming competent at the water start and gybe—two of the standard wave-sailing techniques—will reduce much of the trauma when you finally put the board in the surf, and enable you to concentrate on other aspects of wave-sailing.

Having mastered those basic techniques the

Get the feel of the waves in unbroken water.

next step is to get the feel of the waves. If you are a reasonably competent still-water sailboarder, your first reaction to waves will be a complete loss of balance. You will feel almost as though you are back to the beginners' class again, with a sense of total instability, particularly in light winds. Tacking and gybing will be very frustrating, for as you

Graduate to moderate waves as you get your confidence.

spin around from side to side, the board will lurch to a passing wave, and you will find yourself either flying through the air, or stumbling around trying to regain your balance.

Start slowly, perhaps in a sheltered bay or estuary where the ocean rollers are broken down to a modest surge. Once you get the board going you will find that retaining your balance is easier. It is the getting up and going that creates the

Launching on a surf beach

1. *Wave boards are relatively light and can be carried to the right launching spot.*

2. *Foot on the board, waiting for the right puff of breeze.*   3. *Sail pulled in, step aboard and away.*

problem, as also does gybing. But practise makes perfect, so spend a lot of time practising gybing until you feel quite confident, then drop into the water and practise your water starts.

When your confidence begins to build and your sense of balance stabilises, start looking for bigger waves. A good practice area is in the wash of passing boats, particularly large craft such as ferries or freighters. Stay well away from the vessel, of course, but get into position so that as the wash approaches, you can sail the board up and over it. By heading towards the vessel and taking the wash head on you will get the feel of sailing out from a beach, head-on to the waves. Running in the same direction as the vessel you will feel the surge of the wash wave as it moves up under your board from behind, just like riding a surf wave back to the beach.

The big step, then, is to head off for a surf beach. Be prepared for many frustrating disappointments, for it is a big step from the wash of a ship to the breaking waves on a surf beach. If it is possible to practice on larger waves without putting off from a beach, do so. Heading out to sea from an estuary or harbour can sometimes provide this situation. But if it must be a beach, then look for the quietest corner of the quietest surf beach in your area.

Launching on a surf beach

The lighter boards used for wave-sailing can often be rigged and carried down to the water as a single unit. While moving down towards the waves, you should asses the wind situation, for it is going to play a big part in the success or otherwise of your sail. Ideally, the wind should be across the beach so that you can reach directly out into the surf. This will also make the beach launch easier.

There are a number of methods of launching from a beach, much depending on the type of waves you will encounter. A general method widely used on beaches with moderate breaking waves is as follows.

1. Carry the board and rig down the beach to the water's edge and wait for the next broken wave to surge up to you. If you have a daggerboard, make sure it is totally retracted.

2. Place the board in the water with the bow pointing to seaward and the rig raised. Stand in the water on the windward side, allowing the sail to luff freely. The turbulence of water from the waves will swirl the board around, so keep it aligned in the start position by pushing on the mast to turn the bow away from the wind and pulling on the mast to bring the bow into the wind.

3. Prepare for take-off, watching the approach of a suitable wave. Hold the mast with the forward hand and as the board lifts to the surge of the wave, raise the rig, step aboard and sheet on with the back hand.

4. If there is sufficient water for the board to move and you have everything under control, you will start to sail. In light winds you will need to move forward on the board to prevent the tail sinking. In strong wind, get your feet in the straps as quickly as possible. Brace yourself and prepare the board for the next oncoming wave.

1. Sail pulled over, leg up on the board.

2. Lift the sail, paddle with your free foot.

Water start

The water start is essential when you take a spill out from the beach. It is a difficult manoeuvre with waves breaking all around you, so the beach start is more common for getting under way in shallow water. However, as mentioned in the section on preparing for wave-sailing, the water start is one of the most commonly used techniques, so you will need to be well practised at it. Water start routines vary a little, but the basic procedure is as follows.

1. Move the rig around in the water until the mast lies on the windward side of the board, with the leech towards the wind. Manoeuvre the board into the normal across-wind starting position. You may need to swim the rig around the board or flip it over to get into the start position.

2. Get yourself onto the windward side, and grasp the mast well up towards the top, raising it a little to let the wind just lift it. Gradually slide your hands down the mast until they are positioned near the boom, still keeping the rig just clear of the water, but elevating your body so your legs are near the board.

3. Heave your back leg up onto the board and get your foot into the rear strap. You may have to raise the rig a little to give you leverage. As you become more skilled you can use the wind in the rig to lift you.

4. Raise the rig so that the wind can get underneath. As you start to lift out of the water, pump the sail and tread water with your front foot to give more lift.

5. As the wind lifts the rig into the sailing position and the board begins to move, put your front foot in the straps and sail off.

6. Since you will already be out among the waves, immediately prepare to ride the next wave. It goes without saying that this start requires good reflexes and a lot of practise!

A word of warning when starting near the beach—watch out for your skeg! A fast receding wave or a shallow trough between waves close-in

---

3. And away...

to the beach may cause the skeg or daggerboard to touch bottom with disastrous results. They may be broken off and even the rig or board damaged if the grounding results in a nasty fall in the path of an oncoming wave. Keep an eye constantly on the water or you will damage a lot of gear before you get the hang of sailing out from an ocean beach.

If you fall in the white water you should get the sail and rig out of the water as quickly as possible to prevent it being filled by the next onrushing wave and digging into the sand.

Sailing out through surf

Once you have made your start, you must concentrate immediately on getting through the waves ahead. At first it will be mostly white water with low, broken crests, and these should not give you too much trouble. Get the nose of the board up as each wave approaches, and brace your body against the sudden stop which you will experience as the board tackles the broken water. Even at this early stage, it is worth bearing away a little in the troughs and heading up just as you reach a wave, for the speed you gain with this tactic will 'fly' you easily over the roller.

If you fall, immediately get the rig up out of the water or it may stick into the bottom and bend or snap off. Even if you cannot stand, get the rig up

Coming up out of the waves.>

over your head or onto the board, it will make your water start a lot easier.

As you sail out through the white water you will have time to study the big waves up ahead. Indeed, you should have spent some time on the beach beforehand studying the formation of the waves and the location of the main 'breaks'. A few minutes spent in this way will indicate the best place to launch and avoid a lot of problems when you get your board into the water.

Sailing out should be done through waves which are unbroken or have not yet crested. Try to time your run so that you do not meet a wave at the moment it is breaking. That may be difficult as you get out towards the line of breakers, so if you are approached by a rearing or breaking wave, head off across the trough until you find a more suitable spot, or until the wave has broken.

Wave-jumping

The ideal spot for making a spectacular jump is just before the break where the wall of water is beginning to rear, but you will need to be well practised before attempting such jumps, and in the early stages, an unbroken section of the wave

The white water is relatively easy.

If you fall, keep the rig out of the water.

will be safer. You can graduate along the wave as you become more proficient, jumping steeper rearing wave faces as you become more skilled, until you can confidently take a run at the 'wall' just in front of the break.

Apart from timing your run to the right spot on the wave, a critical factor involved in wave-jumping is the speed of your board. At the moment it races up the face of the wave, your board must be moving at maximum speed, so prior to your run you need to get it moving well. This is done by bearing away from the wind a little, ideally sailing on a broad reach if possible. From here the jumping manoeuvre is as follows.

1. Make sure your feet are well secured in the straps. Prepare yourself mentally as well as physically for the jump. If at any time you are unhappy with the way things are going, ease

Getting out through the broken waves.

out your back hand, luff the sail and the board will simply flop down the back of the wave.

2. As you race up the face of the wave, sheet in and push down on the leeward rail with your back foot. As the board leaves the top of the wave, lift your legs to pull the tail of the board clear of the water.

3. Ease off with the sheet hand and allow the sail to luff while you are airborne to prevent being blown over. With practice you will learn to control the board in the air in the same manner as you do in the water.

4. Straighten your legs as the board begins to drop to ensure a tail-first landing, keeping the sail sheeted out a little. Bend your knees to absorb the landing impact, sheet on, bear away and sail on to the next wave.

Wave jumping

1. Watch the approach of the wave.
2. Sheet on, bear away and up the face...and over.

It takes a lot of practice and experience to become a proficient wave-jumper. Of first importance is to master completely the control of your board in the moderate waves inshore. Then develop the basic wave jumping routine.

Bear away—head up—jump. Bear away—head up—jump.

It will not be long before you are literally flying through the air with the greatest of ease!

Incidentally, maintaining full control during a jump is usually only possible on low to moderate waves. Once you start jumping high, it will be very difficult to retain control. You will get the measure of your limitations as you progress through jumps of increasing power.

Remember one important thing when making high jumps—if you lose control of your board, kick your feet out of the straps and let go the boom so that you can drop clear of the rig and avoid possible injury.

Selecting the right spot to jump.

Surfing back in

Coming back in through the waves provides the opportunity to catch a wave and surf in to the beach. Like wave-jumping on the way out, this is a high-adrenalin aspect of wave-sailing. Also like wave-jumping, it requires a great deal of practice and skill if you are to achieve the enormous thrills without the disastrous and sometimes dangerous, spills.

As with sailing out from the beach, sailing back is a progressive activity. When you turn the board well out beyond the break, you will have a number of round-backed waves or swells to ride before you get to the break and start surfing. These swells are ideal for getting into the wave-catching groove in good time to take the first rearing wave of the break.

As you sail shorewards, you will be lifted up by a following wave and carried forward at increasing speed. Sheet out until you feel that you have got the wave, then sheet in and head across the face at an angle. If you are not ready to make your run in, then continue to traverse the wave until it begins to rear up, or else get up speed on the traverse, head up and jump back over the crest.

If you intend to surf the wave in, traverse across the face until it rears up ready to break then bear away down the face and pick up speed. As you gain skill, you will be able to hold the board in position on the face of the wave just ahead of the break and race for the shore until the wave breaks and you are in white water. Watch out for the rush of wind that comes with every breaking wave or you may find it literally bowling you over!

Tacking and gybing

These manoeuvres, although basically the same in rough or smooth water, take on an added dimension when carried out in the big waves of an ocean beach. Tacking is impossible with a sinker board, so as a general rule, changing tack when wave-sailing means gybing.

Gybing can be very spectacular and is mostly performed on the front face of a wave. A fast type of action, such as a carve or flare gybe, will produce spectacular results. However a great deal of practise will be necessary to perfect manoeuvres such as this, for they can be fairly dramatic even in still water. Among big waves they are even more dramatic and very demanding.

∧ *Riding the crest right.*

Flare and carve gybes are somewhat similar, the basic routine being as follows.

1. Pick a spot between the waves with a bit of room to manoeuvre.
2. Move the board onto a broad reach. Move towards the back of the board so the tail sinks and the bow lifts. Press down on the windward rail.
3. When the board is almost sailing clew first transfer your back hand to the mast and allow the sail to flip around.
4. Move up towards the mast. Grab the boom on the other side with your previous front hand, transfer your previous back hand from the mast to the boom and sheet on.

11. Some Hints and Tips

Using a harness

While sailboarding is mentally a wonderfully relaxing sport, there are times when it is physically very demanding. This is particularly the case when you are a beginner, but it also applies to experienced sailboarders when they engage in long distance races or extended periods of sailing in strong weather.

Beginners who feel the physical stress of sailboarding are usually suffering from one of two problems—their muscles are not tuned up for the sport, or they are doing things the wrong way. The former is the most common, for the first few days (even weeks) of any new sport tends to be tough on unused muscles. Indeed, since sailboarding is such a totally physical sport, using virtually every muscle in the body, you tend, in early days, to feel each muscle you knew you had plus a few you didn't know you had! The only solution, of course, is to sail longer and harder each day until you tune up all those slack, unused muscles.

Back pains, and other complaints which so often give sailboarding a bad name and have chiropractors rubbing their hands with glee, are usually the result of bad posture or bad sailing techniques. Because sailboarding is a physical sport, it is essential to use the correct techniques if you are to minimise the risk of strain or injury. Imagine a novice engaging in weight-lifting without learning the correct holds and stances. He would probably suffer massive hernias on his first attempt and do some permanent damage if he persevered. Although serious injury is unlikely, sailboarding nevertheless places some stresses on the body, so it makes good sense to learn to do it the proper way and minimise those stresses and strains.

However, learning to use the right skills and practising for lengthy periods will not alleviate the strain placed on muscles by long-distance or heavy-weather sailing. This is sheer physical stress and just as any professional athlete must at some stage reach the limit of his endurance, so even the most experienced sailboarder will find his muscles flagging under arduous conditions. The less experienced will feel the strain much earlier, and many a good sailboard racer has lost the chance of winning the race because his arms and shoulders just could not take the strain any longer.

The use of a harness can do much to reduce the stress of long-distance or strong-wind sailing. It can also add other dimensions to your sailboarding such as cruising for many hours along an interesting river or waterway, or allowing you to enjoy your sport for almost twice the normal period. It also reduces the wear and tear on your hands, a feature that will be welcomed by those with any but leather-like skin on their palms. The harness is a simple piece of equipment and its use requires only a little adjustment to your normal sailing techniques.

There is a variety of harnesses available, the most common being a padded jacket (often a standard buoyancy jacket) which fits around the shoulders and waist like a vest and which has a good-sized hook attached. Mostly the hook is open at the top so that release is easy in the event of a fall, but some sailboarders prefer hooks that open downwards as they are easier to hook on.

A harness line is attached to the boom as the anchor point for the hook. These lines can be purchased ready made, or an ordinary piece of pre-stretched braided rope a bit under 2 metres in length will do. The lines should be attached so that the ends are about 1 metre apart and the line hangs slack in the middle. Just how slack is a matter of personal preference and will depend on your experience with a harness, how tall you are and how long your arms. Many sailboarders

Many harnesses are incorporated with lifejacket.

harness line inside your hands so that they are equidistant from each hand and producing the right amount of slack in the line to enable you to hook on without changing your body position too much.

2. When you feel you are ready, pull the boom towards you slightly and hook onto the line.

3. Ease back on your arms, gradually taking the weight of the boom on the harness.

4. Adjust the harness or lines until you feel you have complete control, taking the weight on your body with the harness and using your arms only to make adjustments to the rig as wind changes demand.

5. As you gain confidence, try different sailing positions, adjusting the harness lines to suit. If at any time you feel yourself being pulled over, bend your knees, let go the boom and flip the line out of the hook.

6. When tacking or gybing, release the harness line in good time, change tack and hitch on to the other side. As you gain experience you will get to know the settings for the lines for different sailing conditions without the need for trial and error.

A harness rigged and ready to use.

adjust the ends of the harness line while sailing to increase or decrease the amount of slack. Quite a lot of trial and error will be required before you get a harness rigged to provide complete comfort and ease of use.

You need to be reasonably experienced at sailboarding before trying out a harness, for it can tend to upset your balance a little. Make your first attempt in a nice, steady, moderate breeze, not a gusty, fluky wind, and set the board sailing on a reach. The harness lines should be rigged on the booms and your thorax regions comfortably ensconced in the harness vest. The procedure then is as follows.

1. Get the board sailing easily on a reach, moving your hands to the most comfortable position on the boom. Adjust the ends of the

Self-rescue

Emergencies are not common on sailboards. But if an emergency does arise and you are not prepared for it, what began as a pleasant afternoon sail can very quickly turn into a nightmare. The factors which cause most emergencies with sailboards are related to inexperience and gear failure. A novice sailboarder may be blown out to sea and unable to get the board back to the beach, or gear failure may occur during a long sail and even an experienced sailboarder may find himself stranded. Knowing what to do should such emergencies arise can mean the difference between getting home quickly and comfortably and not getting home at all.

Inexperienced sailboarders can avoid being blown out to sea by being cautious and applying commonsense. It goes without saying that if the wind is blowing off the beach it will blow a disabled craft farther from the shore, and if you find yourself unable to sail back against the wind, then your sailboard will become a disabled craft and you will be blown out to sea.

Apart from the wind direction, bear in mind that the wind strength can change quickly. While you may have been quite capable of working back against the strength of breeze on which you sailed out from the shore, a sudden increase in the wind strength can leave you stranded well out from the beach and drifting farther out each time you attempt to get the rig up and sail back.

By being cautious and staying well within your limits, the chances are that even if you are not able to sail back to the shore, you will still be close enough to call for assistance, or to paddle your board back. Commonsense tells you not to go too far out until you are totally confident in your ability to get back, just as it tells a new swimmer not to venture into deep water until he or she has developed a good swimming ability.

Gear failure is another thing, of course. Providing you carry out the routine checks described in Chapter 7, your gear should be in good condition and you will have taken every reasonable precaution against the possibility of something coming adrift. No-one can predict the possibility of gear failure, and when it happens, it always seems to happen somewhere well out of reach of assistance. The only procedure then is to follow the self-rescue routine to get yourself home.

Assume that, for whatever reason, you are stranded way out from the shore and unable to get back. You have tried attracting attention by waving with your arms above your head, but to no avail. No-one has seen you. Probably no-one will miss you, at least for some time, and it is getting cold, blustery and miserable. The procedure for self-rescue, then, is as follows.

1. Let the rig fall in the water. Unstep the mast and drag the boom up onto the board. Undo the outhaul, the inhaul and the uphaul.
2. Take off the boom and lay it on the board.
3. Take the battens out of the sail and roll it tightly around the mast. Bring the mast up onto the board.

Windward boat (far) gives way to leeward (near).

4. Use the uphaul or one of the other pieces of line to lash together the various parts of the rig. If you have enough rope also lash the rig around the board.
5. Lie flat on your tummy on top of the lashed rig and start to paddle with both arms towards the nearest shore.

Sailboards are usually quite easy to paddle and can make good progress even through a choppy sea. If you get tired, take a spell, but **NEVER LEAVE THE BOARD.**   Not under any circumstances, for no matter how close the shore may appear, it is always farther away than you think, and there are unseen currents and dangers just waiting for you to leave the board. The board has good flotation features and will keep you afloat for hours, even days. Certainly much longer than you could remain afloat without it. Likewise, if rescuers are out looking for you, it will be much easier for them to spot a board and occupant than a small head in the water.

If you start to feel desperately cold and there is a risk of hypothermia, unroll the sail, disconnect the downhaul, unsleeve the sail from the mast and wrap it round you. Although not as good as a wetsuit, the sail material is fairly windproof and will enable you to conserve your body heat.

If the wind and waves are directly ahead, you will find paddling across them easier than trying to butt straight into them. Much depends on the location of the shore, of course, but always try to avoid a direct confrontation with choppy waves for although you will make progress, the effort will tire you much more quickly than when you are heading across them at an angle.

Rules of the road

Just as there are rules designed to prevent collisions between vehicles on the roads, there are also rules to prevent collisions between vessels on the water. As with the road rules, rules on the water must be strictly obeyed if accidents are to be avoided, and severe penalties are prescribed for infringement of these rules. While there are local rules which apply to individual waterways, the major rules for preventing collision at sea are

Port tack (right) gives way to starboard.

international, having been drawn up by a body representing the leading maritime nations of the world, and practised in virtually every waterway of the world.

There are, naturally, a great number of rules to cover the many different types of vessels on the water, and also to cover every eventuality which may lead to an accident. Sailboards must follow the rules laid down for yachts and other sailcraft and these are governed mainly by the relative direction of the wind. There are far too many rules to learn by heart, so all sailboarders should have in their possession a rule book—usually produced by local authorities—with the full range of international rules. The rules which apply to every-day sailing must be memorised, for you will have litle opportunity to refer to a book when sailing into a collision situation.

Applying the rules means applying common-sense. While there is a rule which states that the vessel which has right of way must hold a steady course and speed, it follows that a somewhat liberal interpretation is required in certain circumstances. For example, a sailboarder would be crazy to try to make a giant container ship give way, even if the sailboard had legal right of way. Big ships cannot be stopped quickly, nor can they be easily manoeuvred, whereas a sailboard can be tacked around in a matter of seconds. The sailboarder attempting to force his right of way over a big ship would almost certainly fall into the category illustrated by the jingle:

'He was right, quite right, as he died that day, Insisting on his right of way...'

The principlé right of way rules, as applied to sailboards are as follows.

1. A sailboard is on a *starboard tack* when it has the wind coming over the right or starboard side. Similarly a sailboard with the wind coming over its port or left side is said to be on a *port tack.*

2. When two sailboards are approaching on different tacks, the sailboard on port tack

Rider coming in has right of way.

must give way to the sailboard on starboard tack.

3. When both are on the same tack, the sailboard which gets the wind first (the windward board) must keep clear of the other sailboard.

4. A sailboard has right of way over a power craft unless the power craft has special dispensation (such as ferries, freighters) and indicates this with a special signal.

5. When a sailboard is overtaking any other craft (and this even means power craft), the sailboard must give way.

Remember that these are only relevant international rules. There are local rules in most waterways which supplement the international rules. These relate to such things as the operation of sailboards in swimming areas, any water areas that are out of bounds to sailboards, the use of lifejackets, etc., etc. Your obligation as a sailboard rider is to know the rules which apply to you and to put them into practice when you are

Wave-riding rules may be different to standard rules.

using your board. If in doubt, ask the maritime authority controlling the waterway in which you intend to sail.

Wave-sailing rules

Typical of special rules for special conditions are the rules which apply when wave-sailing. Although not laid down by an international authority, there are basic safety rules for sailing in surf which must be learned and applied.

1. The sailboarder riding in towards the shore has right of way over a sailboarder sailing out to sea.

2. When both are riding the same wave in, the sailboarder nearest the break has the right of way.

3. When both are on different waves, the sailboarder on the wave farthest from shore has right of way.

4. Sailboarders must give way to surfers when danger of a collision exists.

Maintenance

Nothing is maintenance-free, and although modern materials used in manufacturing sailboards are as close to maintenance-free as possible, there are still a few basic chores required if the gear is to be kept in good, serviceable condition. Most boards are constructed of a polyethylene or fibreglass casing around a synthetic foam blank, and thus everyday care means only hosing them off with fresh water and protecting them from sunlight when not in use. To maintain the 'showroom finish' and keep the board looking as new, use a fibreglass polish on occasions. Application of this type of polish, plus a good input of 'elbow grease' will remove most marks and restore faded surfaces.

Hosing-off is easy, for there is always a freshwater hose somewhere to give the board a quick wash off when you have finished sailing for the day. If not, the board will not deteriorate in the time in takes to get home, and in any case, some boardriders consider this routine unnecessary. You will not see many boards disintegrating through lack of a freshwater wash. If there is oil

Sailboards keep clear of surfboards.

or chemical slime in the water, and some has stuck to the board, then the the need for a wash is more important, perhaps with a detergent or even the polish mentioned above.

Protecting the synthetic surface from sunlight is important, for constant exposure to the sun's rays can damage the surface material over a long period of time. Some sailboarders have sleeves or bags into which they slide the board after its freshwater wash, and this provides good protection. The sails are particularly vulnerable and the bright colours which are such an attractive feature of many sailboard sails, will fade quickly if exposed to too much sunlight.

A bag for the mast and sail or for the sail alone is a worthwhile investment, and the extra work involved in packing and unpacking the sail into its bag pays off in terms of long life and preservation of the sail colours. The sail should be hosed off with fresh water, particularly if it has been in salt water, and dried before folding (or rolling around the mast) and stowing away in its bag.

Repair

Small repairs to sailboards and their rig can be carried out by amateurs, although any major work should be left to professionals, for both fibreglass and polyethylene should be used under strictly controlled conditions if they are to have a long and trouble-free life. Similarly the aluminium tube used for booms and sometimes for mast can also be repaired to a degree by amateurs handy with tools, and keeping a sailboard in good shape throughout even a hard summer sailing should not present many problems.

Board damage

Cracks and abrasions to the board skin can usually be easily repaired by a resin. In the case of a fibreglass board, polyester resin is necessary, but epoxy resin is best for polyethylene skins. Much depends on the size of the damaged area. If there is a sizeable hole, you will probably be wiser to take the job to a sailboard factory or repair shop. Small holes, indentations and cracks can be quite satisfactorily filled and repaired at home.

Of first importance is to ensure that the area to be repaired is clean and dry. Grease, dirt or dampness will prevent adhesion of the resin, and a thorough clean-up is essential before rubbing back the surface with a fine sandpaper to create a rough surface on which the resin can grip. With fibreglass boards you can use acetone to help the clean-up process, and where dampness has seeped into the foam of the core, a hair dryer is a good tool to use. The success or otherwise of the repair job will be determined at this stage so take plenty of time and work carefully to ensure that the damaged area is thoroughly cleaned and dried.

It may be necessary to cut away a little of the area surrounding the damage. Remember that a good bond is important if the filling resin is to stay in place during hard sailing, or when running aground or taking other hard knocks. Fill the damaged area well, since excess resin can be sanded off when dry. Better too much than too little, is the basic maxim with this sort of repair work.

Washing and drying sails helps to maintain the original shape.

Mast and boom

Mast and boom repairs are often more difficult than repairs to the rest of the equipment. Aluminium tubing, once damaged, is hard to repair satisfactorily, and repair work on fibreglass masts is more complicated than normal fibreglass repair work. Since the most common damage to the mast is bending or breaking, repair work is quite a problem.

If the mast is constructed of extruded aluminium tubing you may be able to join two broken sections with a wooden plug shaped to fit and secured inside the tubing. Alternatively, a close-fitting sleeve of similar tubing into which the broken ends are inserted then pop-riveted into place may be more secure. Either way a great deal of care to ensure a tight fit and secure fastening is essential, and even then, the job is rarely completely satisfactory. Aluminium tubing is not all that expensive to buy, and a replacement mast, using the fittings from the broken section, is the only permanent solution.

Mast bends can sometimes be removed, particularly with the use of a plumber's pipe-bending machine and heat if necessary. However, if the tubing has kinked or the mast wall collapsed, there is little hope of straightening it properly. Here again the best solution is a new section of tubing.

The booms are a more rigid structure and therefore take more kindly to repair work. Since they are held in place by the handle and boom end, the weaknesses induced by straightening a bend in the tubing will be nullified and a repair job such as this will usually be fairly permanent. Damage to the plastic fittings, of course, cannot be repaired other than with new fittings. The cam cleats tend to wear with time and replacement is the only satisfactory solution.

The rubber or composite non-slip material which covers part of the booms sometimes becomes worn or torn. Replacement by a length of stock tubing is a painstaking task, but can easily be done by an amateur. Some sailboarders use the inner tube of bicycle tyres as replacement material and this is a satisfactory alternative providing the tube fits snugly over the aluminium tubing of the booms.

Sails

The most common problems with sails lies in the stitching. Seams tend to become unstitched after a lot of use, particularly in high-wear areas such as the batten pockets. The old proverb of a stitch in time never applies more than with sails, and you should keep a close eye on any sign of stitching starting to go and get the sail to the sailmaker or under your home sewing machine before it runs too far and you have a major repair job on your hands.

A tear in the sail will require a patch, and although this can be done quite satisfactorily by any competent seamstress, make sure you get the correct repair material in the correct colour or your sail will start to look like a patchwork quilt before many seasons are out. Because light permeates the material used for sailboard sails, it is essential to make patching as neat and correctly colour-matched as possible, for even the slightest variance in colour or untidiness in stitching will show up vividly when next you have the sun behind the sail.

Mast and boom come in for rough treatment in the surf.

Security

Sailboards are not cheap and those light-fingered gentry of the waterfront who are always on the lookout for something that is not bolted down, consider them to be fair game. Identification of individual boards is difficult, which makes the practice of stealing sailboards even more attractive. At one popular beach recently, a spate of thefts was carried out by the simple expedient of 'swapping' old boards for new. While the proud owners of new or specialised sailboards relaxed in the sun after a hard sail, other board 'owners' rested their older, worn boards beside the new. When they departed, shortly afterwards, it was the new boards they casually picked up, leaving their old boards to be discovered sometime later by the distraught new board owner!

Removal from the roof of the car is also a popular method of stealing, particularly when the car is left parked outside a waterfront bar or in a car park. The solution to this problem is a length of light chain run through the daggerboard slot and padlocked to the roof-racks. While it is true that a determined criminal could take the whole lot including the roof-racks, it is unlikely that the average thief would take the time, trouble and risk either to cut through the chain or attempt to lift the cumbersome, awkward package of board, mast, rig and roof-racks all padlocked together! Most board thefts are carried out by amateurs and the sight of a chain and padlock is usually sufficient deterrent.

Take care with the chain, however, for it can scratch the car and the board unless some sort of covering is fitted. The easiest method is to fit a length of rubber or plastic tubing over the chain, although covering the chain with electrical insulating tape will also usually suffice. The padlock must be attached at a point where it will not be loose or free to swing around or it, too, will damage the car or gear.

Modern synthetic sails need only minimal maintenance.

12. Building Your Own Sailboard

Most sailboards are professionally made in a factory where large quantities can be quickly turned out on an assembly line, thus keeping construction costs as low as possible. Some specialised sailboards, such as those used for high-performance racing, may be made by hand but these are mostly very expensive and beyond the pocket of all but highly specialised boardriders.

Of course, you can make your own sailboard at home. Many boardriders do this either to save money or to create a board with specific characteristics which can be used for specific types of boardsailing. However, making a board at home involves a different process to that used in the factory where quality control and mass production methods enable large quantities to be produced in a short time.

When a standard sailboard is factory made, the shell is first moulded using crystals of polyethylene laid in a metal mould. The mould is heated and at the same time turned slowly to ensure that an even thickness of the chemical adheres to the mould surfaces as the crystals melt and fuse into a homogenous skin. When the process is complete the sailboard is taken from the mould as a complete shell. Colours are added to the polyethylene crystals if toning is required.

The foam core is pumped into the shell when it has hardened and dried. As a rule, expanding styrene foam is injected through a hole in the nose of the board by means of an electronically controlled injector pump. This ensures that the correct mixture and the correct quantities of foam are injected into the shell, which is secured firmly in a mould-like clamp so that it retains its shape while the foam is expanding.

The foam is pumped in as a liquid, but immediately begins to expand, and will fill the empty sailboard shell in about ten minutes. Excess foam is forced out through holes in the shell to avoid the pressure causing distortion or even bursting of the moulding. The foam is allowed to cure then the complete board is taken out of the clamp and trimmed up ready for its various fittings. Recesses for mast step and dagger-board, and the non-skid surface so necessary on

A typical foam blank for building a sailboard.

using a male former or 'blank' of polyurethane foam. The former probably achieves the best result but is a much more difficult and expensive process than covering a shaped blank. Indeed, if you are not already in possession of the special equipment required, it will probably cost more in the long run than purchasing a factory-made board. The moulding method is cheap only when large numbers of boards are required.

Shaping the blank

Most wave boards are custom built and if you are planning on making such a board you will probably be able to purchase a ready-formed blank. Most surfboard manufacturers make blanks of this type, although bear in mind that a sailboard will come under much greater stress than a surfboard and must be strengthened to withstand this stress. Stringers, or longitudinal strengthening pieces are added to the foam blank to give this

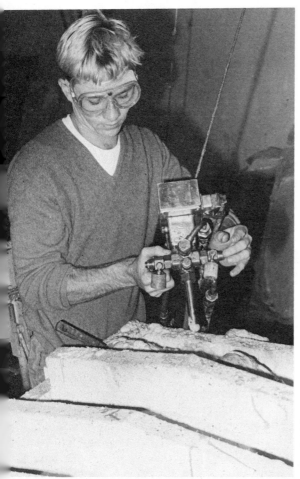

Foam is pumped into the shell as a liquid and allowed to expand.

Shaping the blank.

the deck of the board are established during the moulding process.

Obviously such a procedure is beyond the scope of the average sailboarder. You will not have access to moulds, leave alone heating and turning apparatus and electronically controlled foam injectors. Indeed, the sum total of your facilities for making a sailboard will probably be an unoccupied garage and an insatiable creative urge. Do not despair! You will have to find a few dollars for materials from somewhere, but your enthusiasm and vacant garage will do the job and get you your sailboard at a very competitive price.

There are two methods that can be used—one involving the use of a female mould and the other

additional strengthening. The number of stringers and their location in the foam will depend on the amount of stress the board is likely to encounter.

All surfboard blanks contain stringers, mostly of timber, plywood or polyester resin. If the blank is not sufficiently reinforced, then it can be strengthened during lay-up by adding extra layers of cloth in the laminating process. Cutting a daggerboard slot will weaken the board and if this is required, then additional strengthening to compensate for the slot will be necessary. Your local surfboard manufacturer will advise on the amount of extra strengthening required when you purchase your blank.

If the foam blank is not the shape you require, you can shape it with a surform file, adding the finishing touches with a hand sanding block. The blank must be set up on a padded trestle to protect it from damage, and it is a good idea to wear a mask over your mouth and nose when planing or you will find yourself inhaling a lot of dust.

Cutting the slot

The location of the daggerboard slot will vary from board to board. A study of other, similar boards will give you some indication as to the

The moulds and oven of a big sailboard factory.

right distance from the bow the slot should be fitted. The size of the slot will depend on the size of the daggerboard itself with allowance for a casing or 'cassette' to be fitted. The best approach is to mark out the exact cross-section of the daggerboard on the base of the foam blank, then draw around it a rectangle about 13 millimetres bigger all round.

You can sometimes purchase ready-made cassettes from a sailboard shop, in which case the size of the slot you cut in the blank will be the size of the cassette to be fitted. The daggerboard slot should be cut out with a jig saw so that the cassette fits snugly and flushes with the surface of both top and bottom of the blank. It should be inserted prior to laying up the laminate, and glassed firmly into position.

The mast step

A similar casing can be obtained for the mast step, which is recessed into the deck on the centreline just ahead of the daggerboard slot. This casing is recessed to the required depth in the blank before the first layer of laminate is applied, then bonded into position in the same way as the daggerboard cassette.

Laying-up the laminate

Woven glass cloth of 330 grams per square metre weight is ideal for laying-up sailboard laminations. It can be purchased in lengths of 675 millimetres width, which suits most sailboard and surfboard blanks. Three types of resin will be required—laminating resin, filler coat resin and finishing coat resin. MEKP catalyst will also be required to activate the resin. The following is a guide to the quantities of each required to lay up an average sailboard.

	Cloth	Resin	Filler	Finish	MEKP
Deck	10 m	3.0 kg	1.25 kg	0.75 kg	90 ml
Hull	8 m	2.5 kg	1.25 kg	0.75 kg	80 ml
Totals	18 m	5.5 kg	2.50 kg	1.50 kg	170 ml

Good atmospheric conditions are required for laying up the GRP (glass reinforced plastic) laminate. If the weather is moist or humid or the temperature too low, the results will be inferior to those obtained in dry, warm conditions. A dust-free area is necessary with no draughts and good light. The resins purchased from your local dealer should be fresh, for they have a limited shelf life and can deteriorate quickly. The cloth must be clean and free from dust or grease or the laminate will not set properly.

The laying-up procedure is as follows.

1. Run a strip of broad masking tape around the underside of the foam blank about 30 mm in from the edge.

2. Drape a 4 metre length of 330 gm/m² cloth on the top side of the blank and trim it with scissors so that approximately 50 mm of cloth hangs over all edges. Cut a slot in the cloth and shape it to fall neatly over the bow.

3. Mix the required amount of MEKP with laminating resin (usually about 8 ml of MEKP to each 0.5 kg of resin), and add a tint if required. Stir thoroughly, then pour a large 'pool' of the resin onto the centre of the cloth-covered board. Spread with a squeegee so that the resin covers the cloth evenly.

4. Soak the overhanging edges thoroughly with resin and press them up onto the underside of the blank.

5. Repeat the procedure three times, each time saturating the cloth so that the resin soaks through to the previous layers, thus bonding all four layers together.

6. When the resin has almost cured, turn the board over and trim off the overlap at the masking tape. Remove the masking tape at the same time.

7. Repeat the procedure on the other side of the board, this time using only two layers of cloth.

8. When the resin has cured, cut out the centreboard slot, using a little laminating cloth and resin to ensure the edges are well bonded to the board laminate.

9. Apply the filler coat to each surface in turn, using a soft bristle brush. The underside is coated first, and any drips or runs removed before they harden.

10. When the filler coat is completely cured, sand back all surfaces carefully using a machine sander and finishing with a hand sanding block. Garnet paper of about 180 grit should be used for finishing. Use a mask when sanding to avoid inhalation of the resin dust.

11. Remove all dust and wipe the board with a dry rag. Apply masking tape to the underside as before then apply a coat of finishing resin thinly and evenly across the top of the board. When it has gelled, remove the masking tape.

12. When the finishing coat on the top is completely cured, invert the board and apply a similar coat to the underside, using masking tape to catch the drips.

13. The completely cured job can be polished to give it a showroom finish. The skeg or skegs are usually purchased separately and tap-screwed into the bottom of the board.

The quality of the finished board will depend mainly on the work carried out after the filler coat has been applied, for it is here that the bumps and uneven surfaces are removed. Providing the sanding has been adequate, the finishing coat will give a hard, durable, first-class finish to the job which will be equal to any turned out in a professional workshop.

The mast, booms and sail

It is virtually impossible for an amateur to make the mast, booms and sail with any degree of success. The fibreglass (or aluminium) mast is machine made although some degree of success might be obtained using an aluminium extruded section for the mast. The boom ends are injected plastic mouldings and although substitutes can be made at home they are rarely as successful as the factory-made job. The sail is professionally cut and quite beyond the scope of anyone but an experienced sailmaker.

The rig is best purchased ready-made.

Glossary

Abeam At right angles to the line of the board

Aft Behind. Towards the back

Back to Back A freestyle sailing technique

Barging Illegal tactic at the start of a race

Batten Stiffener placed in the leech of a sail

Beam Same as abeam. Also the width of the board

Beam reach Sailing with the wind abeam

Bear away Turn away from the wind

Beating Tacking or zig-zagging into the wind

Boom The spar that stretches the sail outwards from the mast

Bow Front end of the board

Bowline A non-slip loop tied in a rope

Broad reach Sailing with the wind behind the beam

CLR Centre of Lateral Resistance

C of E, or CE Centre of Effort

Cleat Fitting which secures a rope in place

Clew Rear corner of the sail

Close hauled Sailing as close to the wind as possible

Close reach Sailing with the wind ahead of the beam

Clove hitch A useful knot

Course The track along which the board sails

Daggerboard The fin projecting beneath the board

Downhaul The rope at the foot of the mast that tensions the sail downwards

Figure-of-eight A type of stopper knot

Fiberglass Resin and glass fibre composite

Foot The bottom edge of the sail

Footstraps Fittings along the board in which feet are placed

Forward Ahead

Freestyle Expert sailboarding techniques

Gybe Changing tack with the wind behind

Handle Fitting on the front of the boom

Harness A device worn by the boardrider to transfer the weight of t he rig from arms to body

Head dip Leaning back until the head touches the water

Head to wind Pointing the board directly into the wind

Hotdogging Another term for some freestyle techniques

Hypothermia Medical condition resulting from exposure

Inhaul Line used to secure the mast to the boom

IYRU International Yacht Racing Union

Leash Line securing the mast foot to the board

Leech Rear or trailing edge of the sail

Leeward The opposite direction to that of the wind

Luff Front or leading edge of the sail

Luffing Fluttering along the front edge of the sail

Mark Turning buoy on the race course

Mast Spar on which the sail is mounted

Mast foot Bottom of the mast which plugs into board

Mast step Recess in the board to take the mast foot

Off the wind Sailing anywhere but close to the wind

Offshore Away from the shoreline

Olympic course Triangular race course with one leg into the wind

On the wind Sailing close to the wind

Outhaul Line that secures the clew of the sail to the end of the boom

Peak Top corner of the sail

Polyethylene Plastic material used to make sailboards

Port Left side facing forward

Port tack Sailing with the wind on the port side

Prusik hitch Knot used for securing the inhaul to the mast

Pumping Working the boom backwards and forwards

Railriding A freestyle technique

Reaching Sailing with the wind abeam

Running free Sailing with the wind right astern

Sheeting Pulling the boom in or letting it out

Skeg Tiny fin under the back of the board

Starboard Right hand side facing forward

Starboard tack Sailing with wind on the starboard side

Start position The basic position for starting to sail

Stern After end of board

Surfing Riding in to shore on big waves

Swell Large, non-breaking waves

Tack The side on which the wind is blowing. Also the front corner of the sail.

Tacking Changing tack by sailing through the wind

Tactics Techniques used to gain advantage in a race

Trough Hollow between waves

True wind Wind before it is

affected by the board's movement

Universal joint Fitting at the foot of the mast

Uphaul Rope used to lift the rig from the water

Upwind In the direction of the wind

Water start Sailing from the in-water position

Wave-jumping Jumping the board over the crests of big surf

Wave-sailing Sailing in surf or big waves

Weather The side the wind is coming from

White water Shoreward side of breaking surf

Window Plastic see-through section of the sail

Wind shifts Changes in wind direction

Windsurfer Brand name for popular sailboard

Windward The side the wind is blowing from

Index